MONE

Money with Purpose takes the reader through the challenging terrain of money confusion and helps explain the "why" of misaligned financial behaviors and mindset to get your financial life in order. Morgan Ranstrom guides, explains and helps you to a better understanding about your relationship with money and how to live closer to your values. This is an important book dealing with a very difficult subject. Kudos to Morgan for getting this message out strongly, compassionately and most importantly, understandably!

Michael F. Kay, CFP®, author of
The Feel Rich Project

This is some book! Morgan has written a beautiful and practical guidebook for those who are seeking a healthier money life – and thereby a healthier life in general. He shares his own money stories in a low-way that invites us to examine our own money stories, beliefs, and habits, and provides evidence-based steps to take on our march to money freedom. You'll learn a lot but more importantly, you'll gain a reliable coach who will run alongside you on that march, cheering you on and lobbing in helpful ideas just when you need them.

Edward A. Jacobson, Ph.D., M.B.A., author of *Appreciative Moments: Stories and Practices for Living and Working Appreciatively*

Why are most thoughts around money negative, and why does it feel like there isn't enough to go around? In *Money with Purpose*, Ranstrom confronts personal finance anxiety with reliable strategies for a long-term healthy relationship with money. From zombie economics to uncovering the role money plays in our lives, Ranstom helps the reader build a platform for conscious living. *Money with Purpose* is so much more than a manual for financial planning, it's a guide for living a purposeful life.

Andrew J Wilt, author of *Age of Agility: the New Tools for Career Success*

MONEY WITH
PURPOSE

Receive the dividends of an
undivided financial life

MORGAN RANSTROM
CFP®

Wisdom
Editions

Minneapolis | London | Nuremberg

Wisdom
Editions

Minneapolis | London | Nuremberg

FIRST EDITION SEPTEMBER 2018
MONEY WITH PURPOSE, Copyright © 2018 by Morgan
Ranstrom.

Printed in the United States of America.
10 9 8 7 6 5 4 3 2 1

Cover and interior design: Gary Lindberg

ISBN: 978-1-7327944-2-9

Contents

MONEY WITH
PURPOSE

Receive the dividends of an
undivided financial life

MORGAN RANSTROM
CFP®

Introduction

This is a book about the softer side of money... the "why" of it... the side we rarely talk about because we lack the tools to do so.

Trust me when I say our collective muteness on the topic of money makes it no less important. Rather, in this case, our silence is a testament to its importance.

Despite our cultural confusion on the matter, successful personal finance is quite simple—live within your means. Be mindful of your debt load. Invest 10 to 20% of your annual gross income. Have a "rainy day" fund in place for emergencies, and insure your major risks.

And if that were all there was, I could send you on your merry way. Yet, there is more. How do I know that? Well, very few of us do the above.

It's possible you know some of the basics of sound personal finance. Even if you don't, you and everyone else are only a few Google searches away from a multitude of information and perspectives on how to manage your finances, and most every bookstore has a whole section of titles devoted to the topic.

Yet, the data show that we are not financially well at all. The American Psychological Association published a recent study showing that nearly three quarters of adults report feeling stressed about money (American Psychological Association 2015). If money isn't the number one source of stress in America, it's clearly near the top of the list.

Why is this the case? What else is happening? What's the missing link? How can we overcome monetary stress so that we can live happier, more fruitful and fulfilling lives?

Mental Money Barriers

I have good news and bad news.

The good news is you don't have to be great at math to achieve financial success. It helps in some scenarios, but it certainly isn't necessary. More so, I have seen plenty of very intelligent "engineer-types" make the same financial mistakes as anyone else might, but they stick to their failing plans longer because they are convinced of their own rationality. For example, I know one individual who was a rocket scientist for NASA during the advent of the space program who flirted with bankruptcy due to overspending and terrible financial decisions. So, cross off needing a doctorate in econometrics, mathematics, or even physics to figure this stuff out.

Here's the bad news: there are mental money barriers that keep us from financial success. You see, the adage that mindset is 90% of success is true not only in sports, but in other arenas of life, including personal finance. In all things, mindset is primary, and your mindset, not your checkbook, will dictate whether you are financially well or not.

Does that mean uncontrollable factors like where you were born, your family, or other social factors don't matter? Nope! Your background and life experiences certainly play a role in who you are and where you are in life. My point is, adding financial literacy to the same old money mindset won't get you very far.

In other words, the only way *out* of being financially unwell is *through*, and the only way *through* is to start asking the most primary of questions: Why?

Why do I cringe anytime money comes up? Why do I have these biases around money? Why did my parents have *their* biases around money? Why do I think money corrupts people who have it? Why do I want or always feel like I need more of it? Why do I resent anyone whom I perceive as having more? Why do I think I would be happier with more money even as I think others care about money too much?

What do you *feel* when you ask yourself questions like the above? Do you struggle to find the answers?

In this book, I will go through several mental money barriers that get in the way of financial success.

These are:
- Money Shame
- Instant Gratification & Consumption Brain
- Victim Mentality
- A Mindset of Scarcity

Both individually and together, these mental money barriers construct a firm wall barring us from healthier money interactions and overall financial well-being. Luckily, there are counter energies and ways to positively rearrange our thought patterns.

However, after years in the financial planning industry, reading hundreds if not thousands of books, articles, and academic papers on meaning, habit formation, follow-through, and personal development and fulfillment, there is one thing I have come to see as primary for not only our overall sense of worth and fulfillment, but also our financial well-being—purpose.

Asking "Why"

Most of us haven't asked ourselves "why" enough in our lives, even though it is likely the most important question we can mull over. Of course, there are existential ramifications to asking ourselves the deep questions. And that's great. We all should go there more. Understanding our unique purpose in life is the most important factor in living a fulfilling life.

Yet, when it comes to money, we have compartmentalized our thoughts on meaning and purpose from our financial lives, and, as a result, somewhere between the prayer mat and the office desk, we change.

However, our core values and money are not like water and oil, separating at contact. In fact, money works best when it is infused with the values we hold most dear: love, kindness, integrity, respect, freedom, justice, etc.

Some books seek to give you step-by-step guidelines to become a millionaire. This book does not presume that being a millionaire is a goal of yours. In fact, this book would argue that becoming a millionaire is not a goal at all. Rather, it may be a byproduct of purposeful living or a means to a more meaningful end.

All to say, who you are, what you are about, your goals, purpose, fulfillment... these are what matter, and they help us create the signposts of our financial life.

Money is not an end in and of itself, nor is it a beginning. It is a means to an end, an entity we can use to transfer value, fulfill our needs, live our values, and move further into a life of purpose.

When we live with purpose we live more meaningful and satisfying lives. Our financial lives are simply an aspect of our overall well-being, not to be segmented or compartmentalized. There is not one set of values acceptable around money and business and another acceptable in life. Bringing purpose from the pew to our daily transactions and rituals all the way to our long-term savings and planning can help us live meaningful lives.

When Purpose Meets Money

When you infuse money with purpose, special things happen. Blending purpose into your thinking about personal finance is a potent blend of java. Sip it during your morning meditations, and your day will benefit.

But it's not for me to define what purpose means to you. That is your job, and it will be unique to everyone. My purpose is not your purpose. Your purpose is not your neighbor's. Purpose was planted in us like a seed, even as we were yet to sprout ourselves. Water your seed of purpose, like a gardener tending her garden, and you will flourish and grow into yourself.

At the end of the day, it's not about being defined by your money but about defining how you use your financial resources (current net worth and future earnings power) to serve a broader purpose that aligns with your values. Purposeful money helps you do just that.

Section I

We Are Not Financially Well

Since 2013, the US Federal Reserve has taken to publishing an annual "Report on Economic Well-Being of U.S. Households." The latest report included these alarming statistics: 40% of the US adult population say they could not cover an unforeseen emergency expense of $400, 25% of adults skipped necessary medical care because they couldn't afford it, and 20% of adults are unable to cover all of their monthly bills (The Board of Governors of the Federal Reserve System 2018).

Further, 25% of non-retired respondents said they have neither retirement savings nor a pension while 60% of pre-retirees with self-directed, or self-managed, retirement investment accounts reported that they have "little or no comfort in managing their investments."

The data is telling. The fact that nearly half of the population would be forced to borrow or sell a possession to cover an unexpected expense is a sorry statistic. For many individuals and families, it is not the tight budget that does them in, it's the unexpected illness or injury—a car crash and a few months unable to work due to a back injury, cancer, MS.

The ability to contribute to and sustain a healthy rainy-day fund, or emergency fund, is a primary tool in overall financial well-being. At the end of the day, the Federal Reserve's "Report on Economic Well-Being of U.S. Households" ended up detailing just the opposite. We are, in fact, financially unwell.

Nothing to Save the Day

Savings rates are another telling sign of our lack of fiscal fitness. A good rule of thumb concerning how much of your income to save toward long-term retirement goals is 10 to 20 % of your gross income.

According to data from the U.S. Bureau of Economic Analysis, from the 1960s until the early 1980s the personal savings rate was consistently above 10%. Though many socio-economic factors were at play—a strong middle class, a robust manufacturing base, and company-offered pensions—it is also true that much of the workforce consisted of individuals deeply scarred by the Great Depression, a traumatizing time for many in our country.

However, from the mid-1980s on, the personal savings rate gradually declined, bottoming in July

2005 at 1.9%. This is, of course, the era of big cars, big mansions, and big, ultimately untenable, debts. In fact, household debt service payments peaked in the fourth quarter of 2007 at 13.21%, the highest on record (with data going back to the 1980s).

Of course, we know how this story ends. The ensuing financial crisis and Great Recession was devastating to countless individuals and families. A low savings rate, little to no rainy-day fund, growing debts and a great deal of economic insecurity were piles of tinder awaiting a spark.

As Warren Buffet famously quipped, "When the tide goes out, you see who has been swimming naked." All too many of us, it seems, got caught with our shorts down.

A Personal Anecdote

At age twenty-seven, I was debt-free and making a good income as a financial analyst at a wealth management firm. At twenty-eight, I married an incredible woman who happened to have substantial school debt from her undergrad degree. At thirty, after my wife finished graduate school and we moved into our new house, we suddenly found ourselves with an overall debt load of above $500,000. This consisted of our mortgage, $200,000 in school loans (yup, you read that right), a car loan (an additional vehicle was leased), and nearly $15,000 in credit card debt.

For someone who had never had any debt before, to say this filled me with anxiety would be an understatement.

I felt trapped. Moreover, I was increasingly frustrated with my job and the lack of mentorship and direction at the firm where I worked. I ached to leave and set upon a new path, but I was terrified of losing my income with so much debt to service.

I had trouble falling asleep. I often woke up in the middle of the night with a rapid heartbeat and a panicked feeling in my stomach. I was stressed for much of my workday, which did not help my productivity or decision making, which in turn didn't help my feelings of financial insecurity. You see how things cycle?

At the end of the day, if financial freedom is like an open sunlit field, this debt felt like shackles on my wrists and feet.

More so, I should have known better than to allow myself to get into so much debt. And I knew I should have known better. Another reason for stress.

Which brings me back to my original point. Information is not knowledge, and knowledge is not wisdom. I had the first two in spades—I had worked in the financial planning and wealth management industry for nearly a decade, I had a hard-earned and well-respected designation as a CFA charterholder, and I had an abundance of resources available to me as my co-workers were mostly financial planners.

Yet there I was, wising up to the world the hard way.

Deeper Than the Tangible Realities

These are the tangible realities of money: we spend too much, we don't save enough, we take on excessive debt, and we are woefully underprepared for both near-term emergency expenses and long-term necessities like retirement income.

Yet, the dominant theory is that we simply make poor decisions with money because of our pre-historic brains. To be clear, that's not untrue, and there is much to learn from behavioral finance. But at the end of the day, behavioral finance is a problem-based explanation of reality. Presented with symptoms like irrational decision making, it proposes a theory that helps explain our behavior.

Though behavioral finance is an important advancement in how we understand financial decision-making, there is a problem with focusing too much on our inherent biases. Specifically, knowing that we're financially inept does not help us bring coherence to our financial lives.

Sure, there is value in understanding your limits. And for some, it leads them to seek thoughtful and trustworthy guidance in the form of a qualified and trustworthy financial planner. On the other hand, understanding our challenges when it comes to making good financial decisions can also lead to a sense of apathy. In some cases, it can simply affirm what we already feel—we are bad with money, and there's nothing we can do about it!

13

But that sort of fatalistic thinking gets us nowhere. There is plenty we can do. In fact, behavioral finance itself is simply a tool for helping us understand the situations where our rationality may be challenged, helping thoughtful individuals know what to avoid and when to seek help.

That said, as our modern age has made abundantly clear, knowledge and information are not enough. It's what you do with it that counts.

Today, the answer to most anything can be found online, and personal finance is certainly not unique in this sense. Budgetary tips, best insurance practices, investment advice, investment habits, retirement advice... it's all there.

Yet, even as the barriers to quality information decline, many of us are more lost and financially confused than ever.

From Understanding Behavior to Changing Behavior

So much of the dialogue around money has us as passive participants in our financial lives. We are at the mercy of primitive brains, economic shifts, the stock market, technology, the president, the big banks, the Federal Reserve, terrorism, geopolitics... the list goes on.

In contrast, we rarely speak of money in a positive and purposeful manner. Instead of us empowering our money to support our values and our purpose, it seems that we allow money to either empower us in the shallowest of fashions via rampant consumption, use it as a proxy for our human worth, or, in its absence, we are left feeling helpless and resentful.

It is here that we start to understand that beyond the tangible realities of our lack of financial wellness and even our lack of total rationality as demonstrated by behavioral psychologists, which was always in question despite classic economists' best efforts, there are intangible realities of money that play an important role in overall financial well-being.

We Are Money Confused

Our emotional understanding of money, what I call Money Beliefs, is where we get to the heart of the matter. And I mean heart in a very real sense. For like a heart, which is both a beating entity and a symbol of all things love, there is both a tangible and intangible reality to money. There is the physical entity that we earn, spend, and save, and then there is the less tangible, but no less real, meaning that we attach to money and the ideas, beliefs and philosophies that spring forth from such impulses.

Money, we are told, talks, while also making our world "go round." It is power. Well to be clear, it is also "everything," and we all understand that "He who pays the piper calls the tune" because "Beggars cannot be choosers."

"Money is time," or rather, time is money, and it seems to "make the man." It also happens that money is "the root of all evil," so "Be careful what you wish for."

Where to find it? Well, it doesn't "grow on trees." We know that. We also know that "Money makes money." But that does not tell us where to find it in the first place. I do know that "A penny saved is a penny earned." Also, "One man's loss is another's gain." Does that help?

How to use it? Well, "Neither a borrower nor a lender be." "Don't put those eggs in one basket," and if you happen to have a "bird in your hand," trust that it is preferable to those other two "sitting in the bush." However, "Nothing ventured nothing gained," and I urge you to avoid being wise with pennies, but foolish with pounds. Be cautious because you can indeed have "too much of a good thing." And don't be frivolous, for "When poverty comes in at the door, love flies out of the window."

You get the idea.

If you're like me, all these cultural money idioms leave you befuddled. Yet, we know each of these sayings intimately and could likely add countless more to the list. How can it be that we hold such confusing and confounding ideas about money? How can one entity inspire such contradictory thought? Is it any wonder that we are all confused when it comes to our financial lives?

A crucial aspect of financial well-being is maintaining a healthy emotional and intellectual understanding of money. Here, we move beyond the necessary transactions of our daily financial lives and into the realm of thoughts, ideas, and meaning. How we relate, interact, and think of money has dramatic implications for not only our long-term *financial* well-being, but our *overall* well-being as well. The "inner-world" of money has important ramifications for the way we live our lives and the choices we make.

More Negative Than Positive

Yet, as the idioms show, we are financially confused. Also, like most things, I would venture to guess that we are more inundated by our negative money beliefs than our positive ones.

Studies have shown that we have between eighteen and sixty thousand independent thoughts per day, most of which are subconscious. Of those thoughts, 80% are negative, and 95% are on repeat. And 80% of the 95% of the repetitive thoughts are also negative.

This is likely due to a quirk of behavioral psychology called "loss aversion." That is, we tend to feel losses, or negative experiences, more acutely than positive ones.

From this, and from my personal experience (both in my own head and with clients) it's easy to say that most of our thoughts around money are highly negative.

Take a second, look away from the page, and reflect on your dominant money thoughts of the past week or month. Are they positive or negative? Helpful or despairing? Calming or anxiety inducing? Energy-giving or energy-sucking?

What did you find?

As an example, here's what I have on loop in my head as of this writing: How am I ever going to support our new baby? What was I thinking leaving a steady paycheck and starting my own business? I'll never make any money. We should have confronted our debt earlier. Will we have to sell the house?

A few months into beginning my entrepreneurial journey, my wife and I found out we were going to be parents. We were elated. But we had also just left a place of income security for high income insecurity. And now we had a baby on the way. Given our respective careers, my wife has a master's degree in maternal and child health while I work with many young families, we had a clear-eyed idea of how expensive babies were.

As I write this, these worries are dominating my brain spectrum. And they are doing so in a negative, mostly subconscious manner.

The broken record in my brain isn't helping me be financially well. It drains me and complicates the communication between my wife and me. How about you?

The Broken Record in YOUR Brain

What's the broken record in your brain? What's your money story?

My dad used to proudly tell me that every Sunday night he went to bed anxious that he would be bankrupt and a failure when he woke up on Monday morning. This is what kept him hungry. This is what kept him going, even when he was a "success." Even when he had built his business up to six full-time employees, a bunch of happy customers, and over one million dollars in revenue, he still felt the same way.

This anxiety likely had much to do with the fact that he grew up poor, the son of a widowed mother who moved a litter of young children from a poor farm to an equally poor town. But regardless of the diagnosis, this is the lens with which he covered his eyes every Monday morning.

He was 95% on repeat and 80% negative.

Many parents lay awake at night with restless, blurry eyes and run through their "What ifs." "What if I lose my job? What if I can't afford the mortgage? What if I can't support my kids through college? What if there's not enough left to retire on?" They are 95% on repeat and 80% negative.

Retirees are no exception. I frequently receive phone calls from my retired clients wondering about this president or that president and how what he is doing is going to tank the market. Of course, what they are really saying is, "I'm terrified of running out of money. Can I stay retired? Can I maintain my lifestyle?" They are 95% on repeat and 80% negative.

What keeps you up at night? What's on repeat in your head? What negative story are you telling yourself over and over and over again?

From the Power of Negative

Most of us know the power of negative. It's the way we look at ourselves in the mirror. It's how guilt turns into self-hatred, or how embarrassment turns into deeply held shame.

A few years back, a study by researchers at the University of Warwick and Cardiff University concluded that wealth is not a determinant of overall happiness (Christopher J. Boyce 2010). In fact, social rank is much more important to us. For example, such is our obsession with relative abundance that we would rather make more money than our friends and neighbors in a poor neighborhood than make less money than our peers in a better-off neighborhood.

The Israelites, of course, figured this out a few thousand years ago with all that "Thou shalt not covet" stuff. They knew that peeking over your neighbor's fence, or stealing a glance at your colleague's paycheck, was a quick way to sink into negativity and self-loathing (and nothing good comes from negativity and self-loathing).

However, we are still coveting… regularly, in fact. And worse, science confirms we measure our relative worth by how much better or worse we are doing than our neighbors.

Of course, in our modern world, there is always someone with more. Rich in Topeka, Kansas, is different than Manhattan rich. Manhattan rich is different than Silicon Valley rich. Multi-millionaires and billionaires commonly measure themselves by the Forbes list or by how big their yacht is. And even if your neighbor does not have "more," you will likely perceive them as having such. How else could they look so picture perfect? Isn't that what Instagram is all about?

But let's just say you end up the superior one. You own the bigger house. You have deeper pockets. Is that happiness? Because I have a feeling it is a fleeting sort of happiness. Or not even happiness, but more a brief respite from the voices in our head, those voices that are admonishing us constantly with negative thoughts.

It's the same game, just a momentary switch in theme.

Is money to blame for this?

Probably not. To return to our Israelites, they were doing it with goats and olive groves. Before that, it might have been done with land or access to water or choice hunting grounds. Troy was left in ruins because of one prince's obsession with a "face that launched a thousand ships."

All to say, let's make sure our fingers are pointed at the right culprit—it's us.

So... what's the solution?

To the Power of Positive

We are just starting to learn of the power of positivity. Our brains, focused on the negative, have led to a society focused on negativity. This in turn has led us to a psychological minefield obsessed with neuroticisms, phobias, and the darker corners of the mind. We forgot what brings us light.

What brings you light?

For me, it's time spent in nature, like sitting by a stream or hiking in the mountains. I feel like I can breathe when I'm in the mountains. Music also brings me light... the creative flow of playing my guitar and singing a freshly written tune. Writing this book is bringing me light.

How about you?

Let me guess. You think I'm going off on a tangent. Nope, not really. Think of it more as a bridge.

You see, transforming from financially unwell to financially well takes a supreme shift in habits. I mean, I could tell you to just stop (stop overspending, stop using credit card debt, stop obsessing over a bigger car, a fancier house, a new pair of leather boots... just stop). But I don't think it would do any good.

In fact, I'm not sure framing things negatively works at all. In my experience, habits don't change because we force them to.

A few years back, I was telecommuting to my job from out of state. I was miserable. I felt stuck... compartmentalized. However, instead of listening to these emotions and asking if I could learn something from them, I just plowed deeper into my work. I worked more hours... late nights, weekends. It's all I thought about.

And then a funny thing started happening. I would get distracted on the job. Reading one article would lead to another article would lead to an hour spent on YouTube watching concert footage of my favorite bands.

Distraught, I'd admonish myself internally, turn off the computer and make up for the time by working later, consistently frustrated by my lack of focus.

This continued. I'd never had this problem before. I always could focus and stay on task. Why was it happening now?

I tried everything to make it stop. I blocked ads on my browser (Google is a distraction machine as much as an information machine). I downloaded an app on my phone to remind me to move every forty-five minutes. However, it was as if the more I focused on the problem, the worse it got. My frustration was brimming over.

Sometime later, I realized my job and my attitude were stunting my growth. It was time to move on and be more fully me. It was time to grow up.

I did visualization exercises. I read personal development books. I journaled daily. I envisioned my perfect day, my perfect week, my perfect year. I assessed my values. And, ultimately, I used all of it to start creating a new business that would more holistically serve its clients and community and allow me to be my true self at the same time.

Here's the kicker. As I developed that vision and started moving toward it, my distractions simply fell away. There was no need to escape anymore. What was there to escape from?

Here's what I know. Habits change because something else pulls us forward. Something positive. A vision perhaps. Or a "why." Living with intention… purpose.

Positivity Principle

There is an idea in positive psychology called the Positivity Principle which simply states that if we frame our questions and our thinking about our experiences and attributes in a positive light, we will move further into positive outcomes.

Have you ever heard of a negative cycle? Of course you have. We speak of them all the time in our society. How about a positive cycle? Maybe you've heard of it, but likely less often.

That's unfortunate, because a positive cycle is potentially more powerful than a negative cycle and can do much good in our lives and, by extension, our families and communities.

I'm from North Dakota, where, culturally, we tend to honor the humble realist. Don't gloat. Don't talk too much about yourself. Put your head down, and work hard. There's nothing wrong with that, but many of us end up overcompensating, never smiling at our successes or honoring our unique attributes. As a result, we focus on our shortcomings and the skills we lack. This, of course, is what keeps us humble.

Positivity is hard for me. Blame my introspective and introverted nature. Blame a culture that honors realism and pragmatism. Blame "wet blanket" family members who instead of allowing dreams to take root, anxiously expressed concern to protect me from their idea of pain or misfortune.

Yet, quite often the things we find to be the most difficult are where we also encounter the salve we need to better our lives.

After thirty years of focusing on my shortcomings, and always falling short as a result, I started to focus on my unique abilities. I started to frame my experiences in a positive light.

Instead of saying I lack focus and work ethic when confronted with a job description that hampered me, I said I love being in a role of listening and supporting people and communicating ideas of financial well-being and purpose via writing, speaking and other creative venues. Inevitably, I slowly moved toward the positive.

Instead of berating myself after running an embarrassingly slow marathon, and I mean embarrassingly slow, I said I mentally and physically respond best when confronted with high intensity, skill-based sports. Ultimately, this led me to boxing, which makes me feel confident and strong in my body and consistently stimulates me mentally. This, of course, keeps me showing up.

And instead of focusing and attempting to solve the anxiety and angst that kept me from being productive at work, I started focusing instead on how good I felt after writing, whether it be free-writing, blogging, or drafting this book.

I now know that one of the core triggers of my anxiety is not having enough creative stimulation. The more I write, play my guitar and engage in other creative activities, the more focused and centered I am as I engage in other tasks, regardless of how mundane or engaging they are.

And, of course, now I have a book to my name, which is a dramatically more positive outcome than what I achieved while telling myself that I'd never be a successful writer so why even try.

The Anticipatory Principle

As it turns out, there is a phrase for this phenomenon. Practitioners of Appreciative Inquiry, a group of academics, consultants, and coaches who use positive psychology to catalyze positive organizational and personal development, call it the Anticipatory Principle.

Here's how its defined: "Human systems move in the direction of their images of the future. The more positive and hopeful the image of the future, the more positive the present-day action." (The Center for Appreciative Inquiry 2016)

Put simply, "Image inspires action." (The Center for Appreciative Inquiry 2016)

Shifting From a Problem-Based Mindset

I spend too much. I can't stick to a budget. I'm a bad saver. I don't invest enough. I don't make enough. I can't afford it. I have too much debt. I'll never be able to retire.

I bet you've said a couple of the above statements at one time or another. I know my clients have. I know I have.

Yet, change doesn't come from statements like this. It doesn't result from us "getting real" with ourselves or self-diagnosing. It doesn't result from us focusing on our issues or our failings.

It comes from vision, from purpose.

We know that now. That's the Anticipatory Principle at work. And, ultimately, that's what this book is about—developing a sense of purpose and using your financial resources to support it.

What's your purpose? What gets you up in the morning? What inspires you to action? What keeps you going? Why trade your time and effort for money? Why trade your money, or a higher income, for time?

These are the questions we must ask ourselves. And if at the beginning there isn't a clear answer, we must put in the effort to define one.

Section Summary

- We are not financially well, and we struggle with deep shame around money.
- There are mental money barriers that keep us from financial success.
- We suffer from a largely subconscious cycle of negative thoughts about money and personal finance.
- The best way to change poor financial habits is not to disparage ourselves but to focus on a larger vision that pulls us forward.
- Focusing on this larger vision allows us to shift from money with baggage to money with purpose.

Section II

Mental Money Barriers and Symptoms

Zombie Economics

We are like money zombies, mindlessly drifting through a desolate field of transactional relationships, only focused on the next paycheck, the next bill to be received, the next item to purchase. *Especially* the next purchase. After all, any good zombie is compelled to keep consuming.

Or, maybe we mindlessly obsess over daily stock price fluctuations, or the current mood of the market. The market fills us with restless urges like, "SELL! OH MY GOD, PLEASE SELL!" and, a few moments later, "BUY, BUY, BUY!" From "I'M LOSING ALL MY MONEY!" to "I'M GOING TO BE RICH!"

We are playing head games with ourselves. I call it Zombie Economics.

There is no plan. No purpose. No end game. Just vague ideas or little lies we tell ourselves like someday I'll retire. Or, someday I'll make some changes. I may even win the lottery or something.

To combat this lack of intention, many of us start to see money itself as the purpose. That, of course, is just as dangerous, if not more. It's no wonder so many of us either totter into greed or, if money seems scarce, resentment.

Saying you work for money isn't necessarily an untrue statement. There are financial realities that we all must face. But paying the rent isn't an end in and of itself. Nor is money. Neither of these are real purposes. Nor do they engender a sense of a higher purpose.

There is more to Zombie Economics though. Not only do we lack an understanding of money's ultimate purposes, we aren't even aware of our most basic feelings, emotions and understandings about money.

Like many things, a lot of this may be rooted in childhood. Look deeply, and you'll see your early experiences with your parents or a mentor manifest in your own relationship with money.

Some of those experiences and lessons may be positive. Many are likely negative. But often, our early experiences with money manifest in interesting ways as we emerge into adulthood. And here, our stunted views on money often stop evolving.

To move into Purposeful Money, we first must understand the hidden world of money lying within our early experiences, but even more deeply, in our emotions, our beliefs, and our habits.

Negative Beliefs

We've heard it a million times: money is the root of all evil. To which I say, with a walloping dose of skepticism... really? Is the source of evil really a piece of government-issued paper, or a piece of rock, like gold, or a few numbers on a bank statement?

Nope. But why does money elicit such a statement? There's no doubt. Money does trigger strong impulses within us. Why? And more importantly, what can we do about it?

This question prompts more questions. Ask yourself... does being around people with money make me feel envious? If so, what, specifically, am I envious of? What is money bringing them that I do not have, and why is that important to me?

When you think of money do you find yourself always wanting more? Does it trigger an insatiable greed within? What specifically do you feel is lacking in your world? What would more money offer you that you do not presently have? Is it tangible, like a new house? Or intangible, like a sense of community and having the respect and appreciation of your loved ones?

Or, maybe having or making money makes you feel guilty. Again, ask yourself... why do I feel it is wrong to receive compensation for my work, effort, skills, and experience? What about me makes me undeserving of financial recompense and security? Is it the money that brings me fear, or something about myself? Am I afraid that money will corrupt me, like how it seems, in my mind, to corrupt everyone else? Was someone not present in my life because of their pursuit of wealth? Would it be the same for me? Am I afraid of not being present to someone I care about?

Now, here are some questions for us to consider at a societal level. Is money to blame for government corruption, or is it our own, often insatiable need for power and respect? Is money to blame for global warming and environmental degradation, or is it a culture that refuses to accurately value, in either a monetary, ecological, or philosophical sense, the importance of our natural world?

At the end of the day, the fact that money triggers powerful feelings within us is a poor reason to fear money and blame it for our problems. Really, these powerful feelings about money suggest to us the need to sit with our own inner world of feelings, emotions, and beliefs. In understanding these, we understand ourselves. And in understanding ourselves, we can reenter the world of money with a healthy mindset and the capacity to use financial resources for great good, both in our own lives and the lives of so many others.

Inability to Communicate I: A Poverty of Communication

Our powerful and sometimes frightening feelings around money often manifest as an inability to communicate about it at all. Money as a topic of conversation is a cultural taboo, worse to bring up, in some circles, than sex, religion, and politics. I'm a perfect example of this. I own a financial planning business, I'm writing a book about money, and even I can become uncomfortable when personal finances come up in a situation where I am unprepared for it.

It can be as small as worrying over who picks up the tab at dinner. Inevitably, you might ask yourself… do I pay the bill for everyone? If I don't will they think I'm cheap? If I do, will they think I'm assuming I make more money? Or that they can't afford to eat at a place like this?

Or, what if you can't afford to help with the bill? Sometimes family or friends can expect us to pitch in when we simply can't do it. How do I tell them I don't have the money? Should I just put it on the credit card and forget it? What will my spouse think if he/she finds out? We just talked about how we need to stick to a budget!

Worse, depending on your level of pride (and how you measure "pride"), what if they don't expect you to pitch in at all? Do they think you're a charity case? Do they think it's pathetic that you don't have more money? Well, they're pathetic. So flashy. Throwing around their money everywhere. You could have more money too if that's all you cared about!

You can see how these feelings easily spiral out of control.

Inability to Communicate II:
Our "Secret Shame"

In 2016, Neals Gabler, more well-known as a biographer and novelist, wrote a wonderful and vulnerably written article in the Atlantic entitled *The Secret Shame of Middle Class Americans* (Gabler 2016). In the piece, Gabler spoke to the heart of American financial struggles, perfectly encapsulating the impossible dilemmas many families choose between daily. He discussed these issues so poignantly because he's been living them himself.

Importantly, Gabler's article moved beyond statistics and anecdotes to a conversation regarding the incredible amount of emotion involved in our financial reality. Specifically, he highlights our "secret shame"—our feelings of inadequacy around money—and what a perfect phrase that is for the way we feel about our financial shortcomings.

We live in a culture where we are unable to acknowledge, let alone discuss with any honesty or candor, our own emotionally charged relationships with money. In fact, Gabler goes so far as to describe our financial insecurity as "financial impotence." We don't talk about how last year's medical expenses put us into almost untenable debt, how we feel like we will suffocate under the weight of our school loans, or how we believe we will be working until our dying day because we don't have anything saved. Let's face it, this isn't typical "buddy-buddy talk." This kind of honesty is more likely to see you alienated and ostracized than accepted and empathized with. And yet, it's a nearly universal struggle.

Let's review the facts. Not only are we fiscally unfit, but we combine this malaise with an ample dose of shame and emotional baggage. This baggage has many dimensions. There is the actual financial distress itself, the personal shame felt from experiencing financial difficulty and the social embarrassment that arises from being "bad" at managing your money.

The "why" behind money-related shame is going to be different for everyone. Often, it is due to the earliest lessons we learned about money. Other times it is because we failed to live up to expectations, our own or others. In many cases, it is due to something ingrained in us by our parents or another authority figure years ago.

Regardless of the cause, given the importance of financial skills and knowledge in our modern society, issues like this stunt our maturation, adding undue anxiety and, at times, depression in our lives. If we can't confront our own feelings about money, let alone share them with one another, how will we ever evolve? Are we to spend our entire lives beholden to this inner conflict when it comes to issues of finance? Clearly, there is more to financial well-being than just money and how much of it we have.

Inability to Communicate III: How We Relate

Of course, there is more to communicating about money than who picks up the bill. A recent study found that money isn't the number one trigger for spousal arguments, but it does lead to disagreements that run deeper and remain unresolved for longer despite more frequent attempts to confront the underlying issue (Papp, Cummings and Goeke-Morey 2009). And, with money being perhaps the most powerful taboo in our culture, how else could it be? Even if we don't discuss them frequently, the intensity of our feelings when financial matters arise is dialed up.

According to another study, couples who disagree over money or financial issues once per week are 30% more likely to get a divorce than couples who disagreed only a few times per month (Rampell 2009). Ultimately, if we can't discuss financial issues with our own partners, it is no wonder that everyone gets weird when money comes up at a dinner party!

Of course, regardless of the topic, marriage has a knack for heightening disagreements over the small things over time. But money arrives pre-loaded with so much emotion that it can lead to a sense of brinkmanship we find surprising when not caught in the thralls of the moment.

And these emotions build up over the course of a marriage. A bit of overspending in year one is cute. We're just enjoying each other! A little bit of overspending every year for the next ten is defeating. Conversely, the nagging heard from a more frugal spouse can be just as draining, especially when it has been heard a few hundred times before.

It is easy to blame others in moments of disagreement, natural even. But this impulse simply distracts from the core of the issue. Namely, we have no idea how to effectively communicate about money—not with ourselves, and certainly not with others. Worse, the higher the stakes, the worse we do. (Have you ever listened to Congress debate emotionally-charged topics like the federal debt?)

Here is a tired stat for you. Most marriages end in divorce. Also, we now know that spousal disagreements over money tend to arise with greater intensity than other matters, often spiraling out of control. Though we must confront and organize our finances, it isn't the dollars and cents that are the problem. It's the way we relate to money. Think of it like a tree. The roots of this tree are our dysfunctional beliefs about money itself, while that feeling of wanting to hide under the table when the check comes or the anger that brims over when you look at your partner's latest purchase are just the deformed fruits of a negative money mentality. We need to cut this tree out from the roots and plant a new one, founded on sound ways of thinking and talking about money.

This book will help you communicate more effectively about money. But first, it will help you develop a more positive relationship with your finances so that this positivity can effectively bubble outward, reverberating through your sense of self, your family, your friends, and your work.

Instant Gratification I

To build a better relationship with finances, we need to confront habits and assumptions that are deeply ingrained in the way we think about everything in our day-to-day life. American culture is one of instant gratification—it has been for decades. Think back ten, fifteen, twenty years, and you should be able to recall that "instant gratification" was already a cliché. But that notion of "instant" wasn't always so literal and effortless.

Now, we stream unlimited movies and shows on our televisions, tablets, and computers. We have one-click ordering that leads directly to one-day shipping. There are efforts by Amazon and others to establish drone delivery so you don't even have to wait for the mail. We have endless information at our fingertips, and we are in constant communication with each other via text messages, emails, and social media. A lot of these developments are amazing. But ultimately, the decreasing wait time between "wanting" and "having" is seeping into our spending habits.

Many among older generations are shocked at all the things young people have these days. A couple in their sixties recently expressed astonishment to me that young adults in their twenties can fully furnish an apartment with couches, armchairs, dining tables, beds, and flat-screen televisions amongst so many other things. How are they doing this so fast? With credit of course, I said.

The couple spoke fondly of buying a kitchen table and two chairs when they moved into their first house. Those chairs were the only two places to sit. A couple years later they had saved up enough for a couch, and slowly, they built up their possessions. They didn't fully furnish their house for years, but they practiced and learned a sense of patience that younger generations, myself included, often find lacking.

They were also able to practice intentionality about what they were saving up to purchase and why. Certainly, some of our lack in this regard is due to the Ikea-ization of America. Many consumers have come to value cheap, convenient, and replaceable (yet still stylish) over quality and long-term commitment.

I often wonder if amidst all this instant gratification we miss out on learning to save money and developing the patience necessary for long-term financial benefits.

After all, building wealth is a long-term game that for most people and their families involves decades of saving and compounding investments. Moreover, not only does building wealth have more to do with what you save than what you make, we can also argue that in most instances savings rates are more important than rates of return over the long-term. And in this case, I definitely mean the long-term.

You see, that's the difficult part. If we are trained to expect instant gratification, saving an extra $75/week by packing our own lunch and cutting back on that daily latte simply isn't worth it. Packing that lunch takes time, and getting out of the office with co-workers is sometimes the bright spot of a tough workweek.

We know from studies in behavioral psychology that when we are tired and need a pick-me-up, our brains will favor the instantaneous boost from the coffee-shop latte over the gratification ten years later of having saved an extra $3,600 annually which, when compounded annually at a conservative 5% rate, could have developed into an extra $46,498 in your pocket. That's a nice car. Holding all else equal, over twenty years, the exact same habit would pad your pocket with an extra $122,237. That's a good college education. It's exactly this same dynamic that produces anecdotes of "the millionaire next door" who never made an exorbitant amount of money, but didn't spend much either, and invested wisely.

My concern is that as we move more fully into instant gratification, the delayed gratification of financial discipline will become harder and harder to develop. We no longer hear too much about hiding our money under a mattress. Rather, we keep it in our online bank or digital wallet until it is time to splurge on the item de jour. That is precisely the reason why it's important to talk about the more emotional side of finance.

However, it's also important to take a hard look at our values and how they affect our relationship with money. As you can see from the above, bringing an appreciation for humility into the financial realm may be beneficial for us. Recognizing that the future will offer a multitude of unexpected surprises—some good, some bad—may help us walk away from tempting opportunities that could add too much risk of over-indebtedness. It also may help us develop the wherewithal to build and maintain a healthy emergency fund for unexpected expenses.

Additionally, practicing financial patience may help us become conscious of our instant gratification hardwiring and instances in which it may be helpful to be extremely intentional about developing even more patience for a larger delayed gratification down the road. The inability to enact delayed gratification is a core characteristic of the financially unwell individual. In fact, delayed gratification is key to success in other aspects of our life as well.

In what is commonly known as "The Marshmallow Experiment," Stanford psychologists offered children an immediate reward now, such as a marshmallow or cookie, or a larger reward later if they were able to wait for a short period of time. Those children who were able to resist the immediate high of consumption tended to exhibit more successful life outcomes over ensuing years, such as higher SAT scores and scholastic achievement, better health (as measured by BMI), and healthier coping skills when confronted with stress and adversity (Mischel 1989).

Instant Gratification II: Consumption Brain

A close cousin of instant gratification is what I like to call consumption brain. What is it? Consumption brain is the voice in your head, the anxious urge in your chest that you need, yes need, something now, like now, like right now. Maybe it's a new pair of shoes. Maybe it's a doughnut. Maybe it's a new car. Big or small, consumption brain is that unfocused, "need it right now," anxious feeling you get when considering a new purchase.

It's an addiction, like anything else. When unencumbered, it becomes what Julia Cameron and Mark Bryan call "money drunk" in their wonderful book *Money Drunk, Money Sober; 90 Days to Financial Freedom* (Bryan and Cameron 1999). The authors compare consistent over-spending or debt binging to alcoholism or drug addiction, while making note that they often go hand-in-hand. More, they note that for the binger, the addiction is in control, not the individual.

When consumption brain takes over, mindfulness, self-awareness, and awareness of others are gone. In their stead is a ravaging hunger for more. More shoes, more coats, more tools, more food, more, more, more.

Consumption brain and instant gratification are hard to avoid in our advertisement-heavy society. Personally, my only time of true freedom from it is time spent in nature, away from ads, food temptations, window shopping, and next day free shipping. It's for that reason that unplugging from phones and computers and spending time in the outdoors is so important.

In my financial planning practice, I run into anxious spenders all the time. We are burnt out as a society, and burnout generally entails lower willpower. Willpower, science tells us, is a finite resource. It's not a limitless well, but one that needs time to refresh itself after large draws of the bucket. Stressful meetings, constant email checking, advertisement bombardment, resisting food temptations, holding our tongue, these all take from our willpower reserves.

One client of mine worked in a high-stress hospital administration job, managing a community EMT program. His schedule was full of mandatory meetings, between which he would be nose deep in his phone answering emails. He could also be often found out in the community with his EMTs—an emotionally difficult position in the low-income areas where the program was focused. After work, he would sit on his couch and answer more emails before passing out with his computer on his lap.

His primary coping mechanism was impulse purchases. One weekend a box of new stuff from Amazon would be on its way. The next, he financed the purchase of a new motorcycle. Then, his roof needed work, and a new pickup truck would certainly help his woodworking side hobby. Before you knew it, he added tens of thousands of dollars in consumer debt to his already existing student loan debt.

During our consultation, we talked about how his lack of work/life balance was draining his self-control. There was no time to refresh, no time for spiritual rejuvenation. Every day was stressful. This draining existence was putting him in the thralls of consumption brain on a regular basis. Thankfully, he came out the other end, because he took ownership over his situation.

Instead of coming home after a long day only to open his computer and answer more work emails (before slowly digressing into online shopping) he would do thirty to sixty minutes on his rowing machine. Afterward, physically drained but mentally rejuvenated, he had the willpower to keep the phone off and the computer shut down until the next day. Lastly, he put himself on a hard budget and developed the self-awareness to at least know when his willpower was low and consumption brain was creeping in.

Unfortunately, most of us have no idea when consumption brain hits, which is, I suppose, part of the definition. It's like the ego… you don't even know it's out of control during an argument until much later when you have had time to calm down. Similarly, you do not even know you are in the thralls of consumption brain until after its fever has passed—when you look at the shipping confirmation in your email and know that you spent too much money again. For the financially unwell, consumption brain is just another fact of life.

Victim Mentality I:
Introduction

Though I've been working in financial services for most of my professional life, my path was unique as I studied religion and philosophy as an undergrad. My background gave me insight into understanding how we culturally relate to "The Market," "The Economy," and money.

Within a few years of studying financial markets, it became clear to me that we have abstracted "The Market" as some separate, anthropomorphized entity. It is held up by our beliefs, and it seems to dictate our fate with almost god-like power. Some individuals pray to the market, worshiping Monday morning stock prices like it's Sunday morning church. Others, in a more puritanical state of mind, learn to fear the market and its wrath. Still others are like the diviners and prophesiers, reading the signs in the air and throwing esoteric symbols to the dirt to decipher their message. And finally, there are the Buddhist-like "passivists" among us who implore us to detach from the daily and quarterly whims of "The Market" and simply allow it to work over the long-term.

Though simplifying entities like financial markets into basic beliefs can have its benefits, we have clearly moved from simplification to superstition as a society. The stock market, like any market, is simply made up of the countless choices we as participants make daily. It is not some separate entity, with a will of its own, but a grand reflection of our most basic choices. It is less dictator and more mirror.

I bring this up because it reflects how we endow money with the same sort of power. Money too has been anthropomorphized. Money tempts us and corrupts us like a siren. It gives us power like a king knighting his faithful servant. It spoils us like a bad parent and enables our worst tendencies.

In the most basic way, it defines us to the world and shapes how we view ourselves. And of course, paradoxically, money somehow sets us free. It makes us happy. It brings us comfort and builds up our confidence and sense of security.

Or so it would seem.

Unfortunately, this is precisely what so many of us do; we sell out our most basic beliefs, thought processes, and habits to money. As a result, we become victims to the whims of the financial world. And that is, of course, our next Money Belief—Victim Mentality.

Victim Mentality II

If only I had more money. Ever said this to yourself? Maybe in a moment of self-pity or frustration? Because if you had more money you would do "X" or quit "Y" or achieve "Z." Right? Isn't it something like that?

If only I made more money, we think, life would be so much better. My stress would fall away. I could enjoy life.

Here's a classic—if only I could just win the lottery.

One friend, stressed out over her student debt, said whenever she devolved into anxiety over her loans, she'd end up thinking about how badly she wished she could just win the lottery. Imagine the relief I'd feel, she'd say to herself. Everything would be so much better.

For you, maybe it sounds more like this: If only I had rich parents like (name your friend). I could do so much with it. It's wasted on (your friend). I'd be so successful. I'd live in a sweet pad. I'd travel to such amazing places. I'd give back too.

Or maybe, if only I had received that raise and not (name co-worker). I deserved it, and I could really use that money.

Forget four-letter words: "if only" may be our favorite curse. Historically, I've been big on "if only." My favorite one growing up went something like this: If only I were taller! I would be a Division I basketball player, maybe even a professional someday.

To my jealous eyes, anyone over 6'4" who wasn't a great basketball player was just wasted potential. Imagine what I could have done with just four or five extra inches! I could have been dunking all over people!

It was a great excuse, especially on days when I slacked off at the gym or didn't play well. It also proved convenient when the Division I scholarships didn't roll in. I guess it's tough to stand out as a six foot (with shoes on) point guard, I would say to myself.

Culturally, we love to victimize ourselves. It's so much easier to blame than it is to confront reality.

And in some instances, you are right. Yes, some problems would dissolve if you won the lottery. New ones would likely arise. Lottery winners are still human after all, but those student loans would not be an issue. Yes, an extra thousand dollars from that raise would have been helpful.

But that is not the issue. The issue is getting mired in "woe is me."

Once again, the issue is not whether you are right or wrong in your analysis. Many people have been dealt a poor hand or have had things happen to them that should not happen to anyone. The issue is that victim mentality is not a productive mindset in the least. It wallows us in the comfort of the status quo, instead of forcing us to confront our reality and move forward.

We'll talk more about this later, but for now, suffice it to say that all the best personal development books share one core tenet: you must take full personal responsibility for everything in your life.

That doesn't mean you are to blame. That doesn't mean others are not to blame. It does mean that blame does not matter as much as we would like to think. Here's what matters: you are responsible.

You.

Victim Mentality III

Money has a special way of triggering victim mentality. It's a perfect fit really. We start by giving our power over to money—this entity has control over my life, and I have little say in that reality. Resentment builds when events fail to always go our way. Then, at the perfect moment, our cultural affliction for victimizing ourselves reaches out and takes over our thinking. At last, we are free to devolve into magical thinking: *If only I won the lottery. If only I were born rich. If only I inherited a couple million dollars from a long-lost family member.*

And just like that, our whimsical delusions take hold, and we are led to a sort of mindless and reactionary resentment. Our ego slaps the grit and grime off its hands, a contented smile on its face as it turns in for the day. Another job well done.

The deepest harm in victim mentality is that the rest of the world disappears. Within the ego's grasp, we only consider ourselves, our problems, and the stories we tell ourselves to make sense of those problems. And in the arms of such a narrative, we forget our opportunities, our blessings, our friends who love us, and the people who support us.

Victimization quickly becomes an ocean of discontent unbuoyed from any solution to help stay above water. At its most benign, it leads to a general sense of helplessness. At its strongest, we devolve into apathy and depression.

Victim mentality is one of the most important obstacles of Zombie Economics that we must overcome on our path to financial well-being. It's difficult to communicate effectively about money if we are speaking from a place of victimization. When conflict arises, someone with a victim mentality will lash out, shut down, or both.

Similarly, victim mentality will push us into consumption brain. I deserve this car. I deserve a nicer house. They have granite counters, and they are no better than me. Why can't I have them?

It will also shift us into a mindset of scarcity. In this world, there are "haves" and there are "have nots." And you are just a "have not." Ever heard that one? Victim mentality loves stuff like that. It's wonderful "PR" for the cause.

And finally, underlining all of this, a person consumed with victim mentality cannot know their purpose and consciously move toward it. The sense of restless helplessness is self-destructive, and its purpose is singular, to keep you right where you are.

Of course, some individuals or social groups have been dealt a terrible hand, and one could easily argue that there are, indeed, plenty of victims of economic injustice. However, in my experience, individuals overcome by victim mentality come from a multitude of backgrounds, privileged or not. Though events, background, or just terrible luck may dictate the occurrence of a victim, *victim mentality* is all about a mindset that dictates how we engage with our world. And when it comes to money, wealthy or poor, privileged or not, victim mentality is rampant and hinders the possibility of a more positive and fruitful relationship with money.

We have already mentioned one mindset that cures victim mentality, and we will return to that and add a few others later in this book. But for now, know this…

regardless of your past or your present circumstances, you are enough, you are whole, and the world is riddled with potentiality. Don't let victim mentality fold your cards before you even play your hand.

Scarcity Mentality I: Introduction

Hundreds of years of economic thought has circulated around a few key ideas, one of them being that economic actors, you and me, are motivated to maximize our ownership and consumption of limited resources—in other words, we always want to own and consume more stuff.

There never seems to be enough, goes this line of thinking. We live in a world of limited resources. Your country has limited resources. Your community has limited resources. Your employer has limited resources. Your family has limited resources.

When you read that, does it put you in the mood to share? To cooperate? To better the life of your neighbor? Or, does it make you want to get yours so that you can make sure that you and your family are taken care of?

At an even deeper level, does it make you think of opportunity? Potential? Do you start whimsically dreaming of what could be? Or, do you become consumed with present reality, anxiously assessing how to secure your needs?

People with a scarcity mindset believe that another's success takes from the proverbial pie, leaving less for them. In that line of thought, some see it as better to take first. Unfortunately, many find that once they start, they are unable to stop. This is, of course, where the archetype of the greedy businessman comes from. There is no "enough." There is only "more," and it is mine for the taking.

On the other hand, others manifest an almost opposite reaction. They see another's success as their lack of opportunity. For example, my friend's wealth is a signal of my own poverty. My co-worker's accomplishments signal my own failures.

When individuals with scarcity mindset witness an individual succeeding at something they aspire to, instead of feeling genuinely happy or supportive, they now view it as *less likely* that they will also succeed. Jealousy, self-pity, anger, and a host of other psychic ailments all ensue.

Often, when in the thralls of scarcity mentality, we throttle back and forth between our reactions—moving from a "take what you can" mentality to jealous incapacitation. For example, the individual who hordes money or success is often making up for some perceived lack in another area, parental love perhaps. Incapacitated and unwelcoming in his search for what he truly desires, which in this case is love, he aggressively hordes what he believes to be the financial trophies of success—the cars, the house, the boat, etc.

There is a reason we have these cultural stereotypes, and, though oversimplified, they are often not that far off. That said, I am not recommending judging or sizing up anyone. Bad morals aside, focusing our attention on another's perceived excesses only puts us in a mindset of unhealthy comparison—which is exactly what scarcity mentality wants!

In all the above, the core feeling is lack. What do I lack? What isn't available to me? Why does he have so much? Why does she have everything she wants?

This is scarcity.

Scarcity Mentality II

Scarcity mentality focuses your self-perception only on what you lack. It is like tunnel vision, steering you away from what is present and available to you, whether that's love, support, opportunity, or any amount of financial resources.

Scarcity thrives in a world of overly simplified logic that conveniently affirms our initial emotional reaction of lack when faced with difficulty or the success of others.

Here are a few examples of these faulty propositions.

- I applied to three jobs and never heard back. Therefore, there are no jobs available for me.
- I made nine calls to potential clients, and everyone declined. Therefore, no one wants to work with me.
- I am always overspending my budget. Therefore, I'm not making enough money.

- I have never earned enough income to save large amounts of money, so I will just never retire.
- If I say "no" to this prospect's unfair request, I will lose her as a client, and I can't have that happen.

Ever said anything like this to yourself?

I recently met with one woman who expressed interest in retiring from her career in education. Together, we organized her finances, looked at all her resources, and came up with an estimate of her retirement expenses. After some back-of-the-envelope calculations, I said, "There's no reason why you can't retire. In fact, you could have retired a few years ago."

She looked at me with disbelief. We went through all my calculations together. Then I said, "We'll have to do some more work together to generate a more comprehensive financial plan, but I really think you will be able to retire—it's just going to be a matter of sticking to a spending plan and getting clear on your income sources."

Again, she just couldn't believe it. Ultimately, I am unsure whether she will ever retire. The problem is… she feels poor. And having been through some serious financial hardship in her past, she can't let go of feelings of poverty and lack to move into overall financial well-being, even though the resources are present. Though she is stressed at work and would love to retire into a more vibrant life, full of more time for family and travel, she simply cannot allow herself to do so.

She is, of course, bogged down by scarcity mentality. There isn't enough available, and even if other people somehow manage to retire on similar or less monthly income, there is no way *she* could. Her options, in her mind, are limited.

Scarcity mentality gets its claws in us, without us even knowing it, and keeps us from potential—whether it be an unconsidered option or an unseen opportunity. And, if allowed to fester, it will bar us from something even more precious... the more fulfilling life that is awaiting us.

Later, we will discuss the shift in mindset that will help us move beyond scarcity and into abundance. It's just a simple attitudinal shift that, once practiced and made habit, shifts our focus from scarcity to all that is available to us to support our well-being.

Scarcity Mentality III: The Language of Lack

Money is the conduit through which we perceive our limits. Think back on your decisions over the past year, from the mundane to the life-altering. My guess is money, and your perception of the limits it imposed on you, played a role, whether subconsciously or consciously.

For example, you might have chosen to eat at a restaurant because you enjoy their food, but also because it's in your price range. For the same reason, you might eat at home or bring your own food to work. Sure, it is often healthier, but it's also the cheapest option.

Have you bought a car recently? What led to your decision? If you're like most people, you went to the dealer or shopped online with some sort of budget in mind. Whether the very top of your budget was $5,000 or $50,000, your limits helped define your choices.

Run down the list: food, houses, vacations, cars. Sure, some of your decisions might be based on personal preferences, but, at the end of the day, our thinking patterns are often determined by the limits—real or not—we put on ourselves.

Obviously, showing up at a car lot with a budget in mind is smart. Doing the opposite is a quick way to flush $10,000 down the drain and be tied up in a huge car payment for the next three to five years. But that's not the point.

Because so many of our monetary decisions are framed by our limits, our mental model when it comes to money is to only think in limits. Our spending, our investments, our earning potential, our retirement plan, our vacations, our ability to change jobs—all these things and everything else are framed in limits.

As a result, we use phrases like, "I have to…" or "I can't…" or "I don't have enough…" to define our thinking around a decision.

Well, we are just being realistic, you might say. Sure, I don't disagree. There is a place for pragmatism in sound decision making, especially when it comes to money. But inevitably, money, and the limiting thoughts that surround it, starts to define our life. This is how scarcity seeps in through the cracks of an innocent thought and shifts "I can't afford XYZ" to "I'm stuck forever in this way of life."

Money's limit-based thinking has a nasty habit of affecting our broader life and defining the decisions we make. Moreover, by framing our decisions in the language of lack, we hand our power and agency to money. At some point, we are no longer defining our own life but living an unwanted reality in service to a mental construct like money.

At its worst, this is what scarcity mentality does to us.

I believe it's important to shift the way we think of money by first retaking our own agency and declaring exactly what we want out of life. Only by acknowledging our own purpose and deciding to live the life we envision can we move beyond scarcity into a bold new world.

Mindset is King

Zombie Economics has us in a pickle. Money is pervasive, and the "financialization" of the world continues to spread. A century ago, monetary savviness was helpful, but not necessary. Now, as an increasing amount of our world becomes transactional, insurable, investable, and monetarily definable, "financial skills," as Richard B. Wagner so perfectly puts it, "are 21st century survival skills (Wagner 2017)."

But there is the skill itself—pulling the arrow back just so in archery, a perfect free-throw routine in basketball, or two practice swings before the putt in golf—and then there is the mindset that shapes the skill.

As anyone who has pursued a skill to mastery must acknowledge, mindset is 90% of the game.

Money is no different. There are the skills of money, what I call Money Basics, and then there is Money Mindset. The basics are quite simple in personal finance. They include a sound spending plan, maintaining a rainy-day fund for emergencies, investing for the future, and obtaining adequate insurance to cover risks. These are the "X's" and "O's" of money and ultimately involve nothing that a sharp pencil and basic arithmetic cannot solve.

Unfortunately, what most books and articles on personal finance do not divulge is that only so much of the battle can be won by basic knowledge of finances. Often, we believe people who are savvy with money are also savvy with calculators and complex spreadsheets. However, successful personal finance has more to do with follow-through, execution, and delayed gratification than the ability to solve mathematical equations. As the following example shows, even the best minds in the world often trip over emotional responses when it comes to personal financial matters.

A Story

In the early 18th century, the South Sea Company was chartered as a joint-stock company in Britain. The government granted the South Sea Company 100% trade rights with South America, and the company served the dual purpose of helping to consolidate and relieve much of England's debt. At first, the model proved successful, and the stock price rose. One of our greatest scientific minds, Sir Isaac Newton, saw the potential for profit and invested some of his family's money in the South Sea Company. In 1720, after a significant advance in price, he sold his entire stock for a nice profit.

However, after his sale, the stock continued to jump higher, advancing by the day. Newton's friends and contacts were likely becoming filthy rich, and he became more and more frustrated with his decision to sell early for paltry gains in comparison to the profit he could have had if he had sold just months later. Ultimately, it seemed he could not take the pain any longer, and he jumped back into the stock at a significantly higher price. At first, he was rewarded as the stock made one final burst upward, but then it started dropping.

For a time, he may not have been concerned with the fall in price. After all, he was still up on his second purchase, if a little less each day. But then the day came when the stock dropped below his second purchase price. However, like so many others, Newton continued to believe the stock would eventually recover and make him square.

It's like that with money. The goal line always seems to be shifting. At first, an investor is concerned with one thing, profit. But once the stock is below the initial buy price, profit becomes a secondary concern, and the investor becomes consumed only with "making back the money already lost." Behavioral psychologists call this "loss aversion," and it has led many investors, myself included, to hold onto a bad investment well past its expiration date in the hopes of one day being made whole.

In a bubble such as the South Sea Bubble of the 1720s, or the Tech Bubble of the late 1990s, prices become so detached from reality that they ultimately plummet with a madness and fear ten times worse than the greed that brought them to their unsustainable heights in the first place. And so it was that our luckless investor, Sir Isaac Newton, sold out his entire share, now worth only a small fraction of its initial worth. Not only did he lose most of the money from his secondary investment, he lost most of what he started with before profiting the first time around. Famously, he quipped, "I can calculate the motion of heavenly bodies, but not the madness of people."

Surely, the father of modern physics knew enough math to solve the quandary of personal finance, yet he too was stifled by Zombie Economics.

The Key

When it comes to money, whether scientist, doctor, lawyer, engineer, teacher, or even financial planner, our behavior is more defined by basic emotions than perceived rationality. We endlessly compare ourselves with others, confusing our net worth with our self-worth. Like Newton and countless others before us, we get caught up in the madness of crowds and the cycles of greed and fear. We perceive ourselves as victims of our present financial status or broader economic shifts and cycles, and we subject ourselves to consumption brain and the compulsive urge to consume more and more.

Moreover, our need to understand money and our relationship to it is blocked by a cultural taboo that stifles our ability to communicate about money and assess our very real and human emotions. Fearing the uncontrollable and uncertain, we project scarcity onto our world until we manifest it right before our eyes. Lastly, all the above results in us passing the same negative money mentality on to our kids, just as our parents did for us. Instead of breaking the chain, we have only renewed the cycle.

Here's the good news. It is possible to break this vicious cycle. Money zombies can become conscious beings that enjoy healthy and positive relationships with their finances. Purposeful Money is the key.

Put Purpose First

Our upbringing, culture, the media, the advertising industry, and countless other institutions and belief systems have conditioned us to subconsciously believe we are meant to serve money; not the other way around. This could not be more wrong.

Serving money is what puts us in the proverbial rat race, chasing cheese like we're the punch line of some sick joke for corporate scientists. Serving money is what puts us in consumption brain, a state of need and want. Serving money means we see ourselves as victims when things don't turn out our way. Money, with a mind of its own, oppresses and pacifies us to its whims. And, of course, serving money manipulates us into a mindset of scarcity, a mindset that is unquenchable, and urges us toward an ever-increasing desire for more in a world that seems so limited.

We're lost. But there is a road map, and thankfully it starts with a simple first step. Put purpose first. Focus on your purpose, your vision, your goals, what fulfills you, and then use money to support your movement into that realm. Do not serve money; rather use money in conscious service to your purpose.

In the next section, we will delve further into how that can be done.

Section II Summary

- Zombie Economics makes us mindlessly engage with money and leads us to an extreme lack of intention in our financial lives.
- There are several mental money barriers that keep us from financial well-being and success. These include an inability to communicate about money (both with ourselves and others), instant gratification, victim mentality, and scarcity mentality.
- Mindset is king. Successful personal finance has more to do with follow-through, execution, and delayed gratification than the ability to solve mathematical equations.
- To create sustainable financial well-being in your own life it is necessary to put purpose first.

Section III

From Negative Belief to Positive

Purposeful money involves an overall shift in mentality. It is unhealthy, unsatisfactory, and unhelpful to be bogged down mentally and emotionally by financial matters. And bogged down we are. According to the American Psychological Association, money is the number one cause of stress in the United States (American Psychological Association 2015). For what purpose? What good does this serve?

Of course, there are real financial concerns that may weigh on us, and these should be confronted realistically. For example, many individuals who enter a financial planner's office simply want a reassuring response to the question, "Am I going to be all right?" They want to know if their money is going to last, or if they can dig themselves out of a financial hole, real or imagined. Questions like this need to be responded to with a realistic assessment of the facts, solid math, and clear action steps to follow through on.

But the mental and emotional burden we carry like a bag of rocks upon our shoulders need not weigh us down so mightily. Reassessing how we relate to money and moving more fully into purposeful money can provide the lift to our shoulders that finally shrugs our load off to the side of the trail. With a lightness to our step, we now carry forward, feeling more whole than when we started.

But how do we do this? Often, it feels like the load is strapped so tightly, not only are our shoulders turned in, there is a constant tightness in our chest and an ache in our stomach. The weight of excessive student loans, for example, can be numbing. The same goes for concerns of outliving your money in retirement. How are we to even breathe when the anxiety of personal finance is so constricting?

I believe the first step is simple... conceptually simple, mind you. Mental shifts, like mindfulness, are easy in concept but challenging in practice. Purposeful Money is no different, and it's for this reason that this book is more important than the countless "how-to manuals" of Personal Finance. Without a shift in mindset, implementation will never follow! That said, in just a few minutes a day it is possible to lay the energetic groundwork for Purposeful Money, developing healthy habits for financial wellness.

Start with Gratitude

Meister Eckhart said, "If the only prayer you ever say in your entire life is thank you, it will be enough." I love this sentiment. It reminds me that a simple whisper of thanks is often enough. Forget all the big words, the lengthy recitations, and the paragraphs you were supposed to memorize. All too often, the platitude obscures the core truth: Be thankful. Just be thankful.

Thankfulness, however, is a difficult thing to hold closely throughout the day. How can I be thankful when paying my rent is a challenge? Somebody rear-ended my car this morning making me late for a job interview— should I be thankful for that? Who can be thankful when the world is seemingly falling apart at the seams?

Unfortunately, I do not have answers to these questions. All I know is that an ungrateful mentality can be devastating. In money, as in life, we often consume ourselves with deficiency rather than sufficiency. For some reason, it's easier to frustratingly obsess over what we cannot afford than it is to appreciate what we can. Most of us have access to clean water. Most of us are sufficiently nourished. Yet, it is easier to focus on the night out with friends or colleagues you couldn't afford (a thirty-dollar steak?!) than the fifteen dollars you spent feeding your family of four good food. Why is that? Why do we resent the former and forget the latter?

The answer, one presumes, is found in the cycle of negativity we so often find ourselves in. From this basis, victimization and scarcity-mentality sprout like weeds in an untended garden. So how do we turn the tables, and with what do we till the soil? The answer, you might find, is simple—gratitude.

Seriously, try it. Instead of the negative attitude you so often take with you, try instead an attitude of gratitude.

When you woke up this morning, did you breathe another glorious breath of air? Did the sun rise? Were you able to set your eyes upon or even just call or text someone you love? Do they love you back? Did your car, or the bus, train, or plane get where you need to be safely? Did you eat today? Did you drink clean water? Do you know where your next meal will come from? Do you feel safe in your home? Can you read? Do you have the opportunity to learn new things and grow as an individual?

Asking yourself questions like this and simply acknowledging the joyful simplicities of life may help you feel a sense of peace and centeredness. Next time you feel financial anxiety creeping into your bones, try this: ask yourself the questions above, or a similar set that sits better with you, and reflect on three things you can be grateful for in the present moment.

Often, the occurrences of everyday life are easy to gloss over and forget. But, no matter how mundane they may be, there are miracles to be found in their passing. Don't forget that. In fact, be grateful for it.

Gratitude and Personal Finance

Feeling grateful throughout our day can positively impact our financial lives, resulting in not only a more positive bearing, but real dollars and cents left in our pocket. To start, gratitude is the antithesis of consumption brain. Consumption brain, as we learned, stems from the anxious "I wants" and "I needs" that circle within our heads, hampering our decision making and resulting in empty consumption that never seems to fill the void that beckoned in the first place.

Gratitude, in contrast, is based in the idea that all we are and all we have experienced is sufficient in the present moment. Instead of focusing on shallow wants and desires, or what we lack, we frame our lives in sufficiency and appreciation.

A few years ago, I learned about the power of consumption brain the hard way while buying a new car.

When I arrived at the dealership, I knew what car I wanted, what I could afford, and why I was trading in my current car. However, I did not show up feeling grateful for the basic ability to afford and own a car at all. Rather, it was just another item to check off my list. My poor mindset combined with the sales tactics of the car dealership put me in a state of consumption brain, and I was unable to recognize this or spin out of the mental state.

The salesman bombarded me with decisions to make—brand, model, year, color, and what seemed like hundreds of upgrades. As we went along, my willpower waned, and ultimately I was left in a state of decision fatigue. That is, of course, what the salesman intended because when our brain tires, we make worse decisions. In other words, we are likely to spend more money at the dealership.

At some point during the experience, my mindset shifted from a predetermined satisfaction with a certain make, model, and price point, to one rooted in questions like: Why can't I have that upgrade? Would $25 more in monthly payments really be that bad? Would $50? Don't I deserve this? Wouldn't that be a nice feature on long drives?

Ultimately, I bought more car than I needed, and though I liked the car, a lower monthly payment would have allowed for some much-needed financial flexibility over the ensuing years. More so, I was left with a dissatisfied feeling that was the result of focusing more on what I could not afford than any gratitude I might have felt for what I could afford.

As I reflected on my experience at the dealership I was left wondering: Had I been fully present in the moment, would I have spent less money? If I had maintained an attitude of gratitude would I have bought a lower cost car, or at the very least decided independent of the dealer's tactics?

The gratitude of being able to afford a car at all should have kept me grounded and detached throughout the buying experience. Holding on to what we are grateful for, in this case the ability to afford "X" car, can protect us from the "I wants" and the "I needs" that circle like buzzards in our heads.

There have been times when my wife is driving, and I am left thanking the heavens above that she is driving an incredibly safe, high-quality vehicle. Often, this happens during a winter snow storm or when a solid and predictive braking system stops our car just as another car runs a stop sign. As I reflect on this, I wonder if it should take the threat of disaster for me to feel gratitude.

Lastly, gratitude prevents us from debilitating cycles of regret. Growing up, my dad used to tell me that dumb people don't learn from anybody's mistakes, smart people learn from their own mistakes, and really smart people learn from others' mistakes. For years, I thought I belonged to the "really smart." Turns out, I was wrong. I have made an incredible number of mistakes and bad decisions because I had to learn "the hard way."

In the wake of my more serious errors, I would beat myself up for months. "How could I be so stupid?" I'd ask repeatedly. "What a dumb decision!"

Ultimately, the only thing that could help me move on from my remorse and self-berating behavior was gratitude. I'd say to myself, "I'm grateful for this experience because I have learned so much, and now I am wiser and more resilient." Words like this would help me flip the switch from an anxious mindset to an attitude of gratitude. Ultimately, it helped me move on and take ownership over my decisions, both past and future.

Gratitude is crucial when it comes to personal finance. When it comes to money, our thoughts are so often riddled with ideas of "lack" and "not enough." Gratitude is the switch that can cast aside thoughts of victimhood and scarcity and move us into joy and contentment.

Namaste, Y'all

So how do we bring gratitude more firmly into our lives? Well, we get intentional about focusing on exactly what we are grateful for instead of glossing over the blessings in our lives to spend more time with the curses.

Here are a few exercises for you to try.

Every morning, spend five minutes writing down what you are grateful for in a gratitude journal you keep by your bed. Don't strain yourself. You can be grateful for things both small and large, simple and grand. Are you grateful for waking up? Are you grateful for the opportunity to go for a run on a crisp fall day? Are you grateful you have a job that compensates you for your time and efforts and supports your family? You tell me. Or, even better, write it in your journal and tell yourself.

My wife and I have taken to another exercise. Every night before we turn out the lights, we each share three "gratitudes" aloud with each other. Often, I find myself telling her that I'm grateful for her, who she is, all that she does, and that she has been willing to put up with me all these years. As it turns out, she likes that, and it helps our marriage. After going through our lists, I find that I feel good about my day and the day to come, instead of restlessly pondering what went wrong and could go wrong tomorrow.

An attitude of gratitude can help you during the day, as well. Whenever you walk up to your car, before worrying about how late you are, how you wish you didn't have a car payment, or how you wish you had a nicer car, try this instead: say, I'm grateful that I have the ability and financial wherewithal to drive this car today and that it gets me safely where I need to be.

You can do this with any number of things. I find myself thinking similar thoughts about my house. I'm grateful that it provides a space for so much love and joy. I'm grateful that we can host people we love on a regular basis. And I'm grateful that it protects me and my family from storms, wind, rain, terrible heat, and the trembling cold. And when my mortgage statement comes in the mail, I'm grateful for that, as well, because paying my mortgage helps me stay in this house that I feel so grateful for!

Gratitude can help you achieve goals, as well. For example, instead of worrying about whether you should buy that tantalizing box of doughnuts, say to yourself instead, I'm grateful that I am affirming myself, my health, and my well-being by eating healthy foods and living an active lifestyle.

Similarly, instead of clicking "Buy" on your online shopping cart full of items you don't need, close your laptop and try this instead: Say, I'm grateful that I am executing on my plan to achieve long-term and sustainable financial well-being. In ten years, I'll feel even more grateful for positive decisions like this.

Lastly, and this might be the most challenging and scary for some of us, you can tell other people that you are grateful for them. Tell others that you are thankful for them and what they contribute to the world around them.

I appreciate you. I'm grateful for this opportunity. Thank you.

They all work. Try them. Wear them out, even. No one will get mad at you. And don't worry about what the people you say this to say back. Know that they are likely dealing with their own stuff. And that's okay. You said aloud what you feel. And that's okay too.

Sound hippy-dippy? Good. It is. Get over that fact, and don't waste another second worrying about it. In fact, take all the time you would have spent judging yourself for feeling grateful, and just be grateful. You'll get more out of it.

Namaste, y'all.

How to Cultivate Money Gratitude in Your Life

1. Keep a gratitude journal, and write down a list of things (events, loved ones, material things, the sheer blessing and joy of being alive) that you are grateful for every morning. Make a point to add a couple money-related "gratitudes" every day. "I'm grateful for my paycheck that allows me to afford a safe and healthy space for my family." "I'm grateful I've been diligent about contributing to my

retirement accounts this past year because it makes me feel more financially secure."

2. Make a habit of sharing a short list of "gratitudes" with a partner, spouse, friend or colleague daily.

3. Before making a large purchase, take a moment to reflect on your long-term goals and vision of success and put yourself in the shoes of your future self. Imagine what it will feel like to achieve your goals and simply "be" in that moment. What are you seeing? Sensing? Feeling? Now, reflect on the actions and habits that brought you here. Maybe you are reflecting on the daily habits of sticking to your spending and savings plan so that you can take a sabbatical or retire with confidence. Or, maybe you burn the midnight oil to expand your skills and capabilities which ultimately brings new and well-compensated employment opportunities. Regardless, from this vantage, fill yourself with gratitude for the activities you are presently engaging in that bring you to that future place. Now, reconsider your purchase. Does this move you closer to your goals?

From Victim to Empowered

Even with gratitude taking a central place in our lives, we are still left with an important question: how do we move from victimhood to empowerment in our financial lives?

The answer is easier than you think. A few years back, when I was at a low in my life and consumed with self-blame and victimizing myself, I started reading all the books that I had always been too proud to read before. You know the ones I'm talking about. They can be found in the "Self Help" section of the bookstore. Or, as it is now called, "Personal Development."

One after another, I devoured the greats as well as some more obscure titles, and I added these to my regular reading on more spiritual topics (I have a passion for all things Thomas Merton and Parker Palmer). As I was reading, I started to notice a common thread around victimization and how to respond to it. Here's the gist: You are responsible for everything that occurs in your life. Big and small, meaningful and meaningless. You are responsible.

You might read that as "You are to blame." Not necessarily. Bad things happen to undeserving people all the time. That doesn't make them culpable. But we are responsible. Why? Because events are not just happening to us. We are active participants in our own lives. We co-create our reality.

But, if I'm not to blame, how am I responsible?

That's a good question, and frankly, I am unsure if I have a satisfactory answer. I do have some thoughts though. Blame and culpability are mindsets that chain us to the past. We are constantly seeking answers in the past to define why we feel a certain way in the present, why another event happened, or why things turned out the way they did. There may be historical value to this, but when we allow ourselves to be emotionally consumed by the past, we chain ourselves to it, and we become victims of its outcomes.

In contrast, when someone says, "I am fully responsible for everything in my life," they have made a statement that grabs the reins of their past, present, and future and bravely cuts ties with the mind-numbing blame game that so often dominates us.

A victim needs a savior because events outside of his control seemingly dictate his present, and so only outside events will absolve him of his hardship. In contrast, someone who takes responsibility for all things in his life can overcome challenges and work toward more satisfactory or fulfilling outcomes.

Ultimately, taking full responsibility is about building resilience. Bad things will happen. Outcomes will, at times, be worse than you had hoped. When these occur, you can either respond like a victim would, pointing fingers and obsessing over blame, or you can respond in a more productive fashion.

Repeat after me: I am responsible for who I am right now, how I see the world, and how I react to events in my life. As a result, I am responsible for my present actions and how I respond, as well as who I become in the future.

Responsibility and Money

Victimhood is built into the way we understand
money. Here are just a few statements that manifest
victim mentality. Some may be painfully familiar.

1. Our greedy government taxes me too much and
   steals my hard-earned money!
4. The greedy bank gave me a mortgage that I had
   no hope of repaying.
5. The crazy stock market crashed and lost all my
   money!
6. Johnny was given everything by his parents! If
   I had what he had I'd be successful too!

These statements neglect our own responsibility
and choices. They put us in a frame of mind that life is
happening to us, not with our participation. In all cases,
we have personified our oppressor (the government!
the banks! the 1%! the stock market!) and shirked
responsibility for our own lives onto them. More so,
victim-brain makes it personal. The government, the
bank, Johnny's rich parents, and the market—they all
took from you what you deserve!

But the harsh reality is that it isn't personal. In fact,
it may be true that your government wastes your tax
money, the banks screwed the economy, and that Johnny
is a brat, but the blame game is unproductive. The only
way out is to take responsibility, learn what you can,
and move on. Every second grader learns an important
lesson when they point their finger at someone else.

Invariably, the teacher will say, "Don't worry about her. Worry about yourself."

The same goes for your financial reality. Other than feeling grateful for your hard-earned lessons (we all have had our fair share), it's not about how you arrived at where you are—whether that's bankrupt, broke, over-worked, underpaid, or stressed to the max. It is about how you are going to use the present and future resources at your disposal to achieve a more fulfilling future. Frankly, that is all that matters.

When you make this shift in mindset, you move from the passenger seat to the driver's seat. Put your hands to the wheel, place your foot on the pedal, and start driving. This life is yours to live.

Let's look at the negative statements above that exemplify victim mentality. How might we state these differently so that we take responsibility for where we are in life and can move forward with intention?

1. Every day, I reaffirm my desire to live in the United States and live according to its laws, because my loved ones live here and because I have economic opportunities here that I may not have elsewhere. Because I find our current system inequitable I consistently advocate for comprehensive tax reform. Also, I take advantage of smart tax planning to reduce my tax bill as much as possible so I can allocate my hard-earned resources as I choose.

2. Though the bank enabled me, I am responsible for my own financial choices, and I took on

a mortgage that I had no hope of repaying because I hoped that house prices would continue to rise indefinitely.

3. I may not have had the same opportunities as Johnny, but my path has offered me a unique batch of wisdom and life lessons that I can use to achieve my goals, financial and otherwise.

4. I invested all my hard-earned savings in the riskiest parts of the stock market because my friend kept telling me it was a sure thing, and he was making so much money. I also panicked and sold my stocks near the bottom, so I didn't benefit from the ensuing recovery. The stock market did what it does, it went up and down. I made my own choices and have learned important lessons about life and money from them.

How to Cultivate Money Responsibility

Here are a few exercises to cultivate responsibility around money.

1. Meditate. When we meditate, we move from egoistic games like blame and shame and into a more mindful consciousness that accepts the present moment as it is and can creatively and productively respond to it as necessary. Developing a more mindful relationship with money can pay dividends for the rest of your life as you align your financial decisions positively and proactively with

your core values without feeling stressed or overwhelmed.

2. Say a morning mantra. Consider the following: I am responsible for all things in my life including my finances. I have the tools, the wisdom, and the potential to achieve my goals, financial and otherwise.

3. Move from passive language to active language with money. After reading this book, you might notice how passive our language is around money. What's the market doing? That mutual fund lost my money! When you feel tempted to use language like this, consciously make the effort to reframe it actively. For example, instead of the above examples, you can say, "I understand the short-term risks in the stock market, but I am choosing to invest because this is a solid strategy for achieving my long-term goals."

4. Move from negative money language to positive language with money. Instead of saying, "I can't afford to go to fancy restaurants," say, "I am choosing to allocate my money elsewhere, like saving up for my dream trip to Thailand in two years." Or, instead of "I'll never pay off my school loans," try "I calculated it all out, and at this payment level I will pay off my school loans in exactly fifteen years, while at this payment level I can pay them off in ten years."

The initial examples feed a sense of victimhood and helplessness. The latter examples positively affirm our ability to make active choices that dictate our future. Which type of person would you rather be?

From Scarcity to Abundance

The third mindset of the financially unwell is a mindset rooted in scarcity. Scarcity brain manifests in many ways. Sometimes it pops up as a "winner takes all" mentality. If he wins, I lose or vice versa. It can also be a mentality of "either this or that." For example, I can either have better work/life balance or I can advance in my career, but I cannot do both.

Overwhelmingly though, scarcity is about the idea of "never enough." For those under the spell of this mindset, there is never enough money, time, appreciation, or love. People who are rooted in scarcity can shrug their shoulders at their own impoverishment (tangible or intangible) because there isn't "more" out there for them. Similarly, another person with scarcity brain may earn two million dollars per year and still feel poor. In that sense, scarcity is bank account agnostic, meaning it's a mindset that affects the deep-pocketed and the empty-pocketed equally.

A shift needs to occur. That is, we must move from scarcity brain to a mindset rooted in something more expansive, uplifting and unifying. We need to shift toward a mentality of abundance.

What does abundance mean?

Abundance is the idea that the world has so much more capacity and potential than we could ever exhaust. There is "enough" for all of us, including you. Including her. Including them. For all of us, there is enough.

Abundance is a counterforce to defeatism, apathy, and cynicism. It is an opposing energy full of vibrancy, potential, and life. It is vivifying. It is regenerative. It is confidence-boosting.

If an individual rooted in abundance loses his job, he does not despair because he firmly believes there are other opportunities awaiting him. So instead, he wonders with openness and genuine curiosity what his next journey will be. He might meditate or do some journaling to center himself and to start envisioning next steps. Then, instead of sitting in his apartment, frustrated and alone, he reaches out to professional and personal contacts every day to set up times to meet for coffee or lunch. There may be a situation where he can be of service to them, or maybe they know about a new opportunity where he could use his unique skills for the benefit of others.

Many of his contacts, though genuinely happy to connect, are unfortunately unable to help. However, he holds firm to the belief that opportunity awaits, and he simply must continue knocking on doors to find it. Ultimately, a friend he had coffee with a month back calls him up and says his company is hiring. He interviews, is offered a well-paying job, and with gratitude and the same sense of openness he's harbored all along he accepts.

This is an attitude of abundance. When one door closes, you trust that a thousand open. You see opportunity, ample resources and energy when another individual might devolve into despair and resentment.

A similar story may take place for a retiree who has an abundance mentality. Though she may feel a degree of concern, she does not experience anxiety over the potential of running out of money. Instead, she says, "I have all these skills along with a wealth of experience and wisdom. Surely, I can use them to earn an extra $1,000 per month working part time."

So, she goes out into the world, meeting all sorts of new and exciting people who connect her with all sorts of new and exciting opportunities. She flourishes. Just as importantly, her $12,000 in additional annual income reduces the strain on her investment portfolio and dramatically improves her financial position.

Contrast this, of course, with a retiree whose thought processes are rooted in scarcity. He assumes that no one wants him, that no one will employ him, nor pay him for any service he might offer. He feels as if the world has rejected him and becomes more and more insular. He doesn't go out. He doesn't learn new things. He doesn't share his wisdom with the world.

He calls his financial advisor every week to anxiously discuss his investments because he is terrified of running out of money. Where the people in the prior examples saw possibility and opportunity, he only sees boundaries and both personal and financial constraints.

He is defined by his self-imposed limits, and those limits are caving in on him.

Scarcity says, "I'm just a loser living in my parents' basement. I'll never find a job or pay off my school loans." Abundance says, "I'm eagerly anticipating landing one of the great job opportunities that I *know* exist and that will help me pay off my school loans quickly and efficiently."

Scarcity says, "If I don't compromise on my pricing or values, I will not land this client/contract/sale." Abundance says, "Saying no to this client affirms my values and my service's (or product's) worth. Also, I can more quickly get to that next client or opportunity where my business is appreciated and valued."

I have a client in her early sixties who is in the process of launching a career as a life coach and meditation instructor, a job she could easily do into her eighties should she stay healthy. She knows she has much to offer, and she is not limited by any social constructs that dictate a compulsory retirement at her age.

She seeks fulfillment, and her worldview is rooted in abundance. When we meet, I feel as if she is the planner and I am the client because of all that she teaches me. I am so grateful that she is sharing her talents with the world, and I sense her clients and students will share this gratitude for years to come.

At its root, abundance may seem to share similarities with hope. But there is one core difference. Instead of "hoping" you are "knowing" and constantly affirming the opportunities and potentials inherent within you as well as within the broader world. Hoping for a bigger and better future is passive, as if someone or something else will deliver it to you. Believing and acting toward a bigger and better future is the mark of abundance. You act as if "it"—a job, an opportunity, a mentor, a raise, financial security—already exists. As a result, you co-create that very future.

Some people confuse abundance with being rich. When they hear the word "abundance" they picture in their minds owning ten cars and a giant house on the beach and taking lavish vacations. Though this may be one potential outcome of abundance, abundance itself is outcome agnostic. It is not rooted in the future, but in the present. In that sense, abundance is more a state of mind and a way of being.

Scarcity mentality says, "If I were making a million dollars per year living in a penthouse overlooking Central Park, then I would feel rich." Abundance says, "I feel rich in spirit, and I can creatively and effectively share my knowledge, skills, joy, and enthusiasm with the world around me in the present."

Abundance is not money growing on trees. It is knowing that with pure and grateful intent, your needs and desires will be met. Abundance is not everyone giving you love, it is knowing that there is always more love to give. Abundance is not every moment a happy one, it is happiness in every moment.

When you feel abundant, you feel as if the sun is just about to rise. And like anyone who awakes before the dawn to watch as the sun crests the horizon, you sit with grateful anticipation until you feel the first tempered rays drift across your skin. Then, with your "knowing" affirmed, you appreciate every second of its rise to magnificence. And when you turn to begin your day, you are already grateful for what comes next, knowing that it will be cast in the brightest of lights.

That is abundance.

Harboring Abundance

Harboring abundance is less a journey of the pocketbook and more a journey of the mind and spirit. However, that doesn't diminish its importance to long-term financial well-being. In fact, a spirit of abundance is a core aspect of purposeful money. More so, it can have a dramatic impact on your finances.

Though we often think of abundance in terms of receiving, it has as much, if not more, to do with giving. When you feel abundant, you are more likely to give your time, your talents, your creativity, your skills, your gratitude, your appreciation, and yes, your money, toward purposes that serve the well-being of you, your family, your workplace, your community, your environment, and your world.

So often, we cling to what we have, stowing it away and guarding it as if it will be taken from us if shown the light of day. Yet when we do this, we are dismissing the renewable capacity of much of what we can offer the world. We so often treat our gifts, our talents, and our resources as if they are ponds that can be drained instead of rivers running clearly.

Money, too, is a renewable resource, and there is always more of it to be made. Importantly, there is plenty of money to go around, and, in fact, it is crucial that it does indeed go around. Here too, with our clinginess and anxiety, we can staunch the flow of money, turning a rejuvenating cycle into stagnant, dirty water. When we cling to money, what we fear is the day when our pot of gold will be the last oasis in an encroaching desert. Unfortunately, this mindset is a self-fulfilling prophecy and creates the very thing we fear.

That isn't to say "spend frivolously," but we can all agree that there is no glory in being the richest man or woman in the graveyard. "Give freely" is a better phrase. If you ate a meal today, have a roof over your head, and at least one person loves you, you are blessed. If you know what your values are and live and act with purpose, you are doubly blessed. Give freely, for what is given shall be returned to you twofold. Yes, it might be in a different form. Creativity may be affirmed with money. Charity may be affirmed with the smile of a child. A seed given may be a garden returned. When we give, we are watching as our purpose flows, over mountains and valleys, on its way back to sea.

At the end of the day, there is a courage and a vulnerability to abundance. If I give love, will it ever be received or returned to me? If I give money, will it be used wisely? Will I make more? Is our future brighter than our past? Is there enough?

The answer is I don't know. Yet, when someone truly moves into a mindset of abundance, questions like these tend to fall away. A person in a state of abundance thinks more about what they can give than what they can get. More so, living in a world of abundance shifts your entire reality. What once brought anxiety now only brings the confidence that the world has so much to offer, and it is there to be received if you are open. All that can be extended is the opportunity for abundance. It's here, not to be grasped, but embodied.

How to Harbor Abundance in Your Own Life

So much of abundance is our mindset and the way we feel as we go about our day. When we cling to our fear we block the rays of an abundant sun that offer us the potential for growth, inspiration, connection, and opportunity. Here's a simple exercise for harboring abundance. I call it "Act as if."

1. Envision your perfect day. Write it down hour by hour. Then, pick any day this coming week, and act as if your perfect day is being realized. Of course, you might not be able to do it perfectly, but what *can* you do? If you ache for nature, as I often do, take time to go for a walk or jog in your favorite local park. If you are burgeoning with creative energy, block out an hour or two to paint, draw, or to play an instrument. If your day involves time with loved ones, meet a friend or two for lunch, or schedule a date with your

partner. Do what you must to make it work. Hire a babysitter. Take a day off work. Act as if...

2. If, five years down the road, you felt totally abundant, what would be going on in your life? How would you be going about your day? Now, act as if that moment has arrived today. Treat people as if you were engaged and grateful for your life. Pursue activities as if you were an individual of passion and purpose. Do the things that in the future you would be doing, but do them today!

Communicate Mindfully About Money

From the perspective of gratitude, empowerment, personal responsibility, and abundance, it becomes natural to communicate with our spouses, family, friends, and colleagues more mindfully about money. However, there are other skills we can develop and rely upon as well.

One of my favorite books is *Non-Violent Communication: A Language of Life* by Marshall B. Rosenberg (Rosenberg 2015). It's a wonderfully written book that provides a practical guide for learning effective and respectful communication. Money is a realm where we could use a healthy dose of non-violent communication to help us when speaking with others as well as with our own internal dialogue. Remember, it is just as important to non-violently communicate with yourself as it is with others. In fact, it may be more important.

Using Dr. Rosenberg's book as a guide, here are a few helpful tips to communicate respectfully, patiently, and clearly about money.

Listen and Speak Nonjudgmentally

According to the tenets of non-violent communication, judgment of others contributes to violence. When we talk about money, we must recognize how emotionally charged this topic is both for ourselves (as the listener and/or speaker) as well as for the one with whom we are communicating. Any perceived judgment will likely lead to your conversation partner shutting down and turning off. If you feel judgment arising within you when talking about money, acknowledge it internally and then let it go.

Avoid Giving Opinions or Advice

Often, when we listen to another's problems, our first impulse is to solve them. This does not necessarily come from a bad place; a desire to help is indeed a good thing. But it can bar us from empathy or from understanding our own feelings that may be brewing underneath the surface.

When a friend's or loved one's financial worries or experiences come up in conversation, it's terribly difficult to not insert your own personal biases as if they were foregone conclusions. Resist this urge!

Usually, when someone is sharing a financial issue with you they are not looking for your opinions.

Rather, they are desiring a listener. Offer that space if you can. If not, pleasantly excuse yourself. However, in conversation it is usually better to ask the right question, allowing your conversation partner to come to their own conclusions in a healthy manner. Then offer, unsolicited, what you see as the right answer or solution.

Clearly Acknowledge and Express Your Needs

The main roadblock to getting our needs met is that we do not effectively communicate them. Often, we are expressing judgments in place of our needs. Instead, we should be stating our needs, which of course means that we have spent time ensuring that we are clear on our own needs and making clear requests to another to help us meet those needs. Here's an example:

> As a family with limited resources, I believe it's in our best interest to stick to our pre-decided monthly budget. When you spend "X" amount of money without communicating with me prior it makes me feel unimportant, dismissed, and frustrated. It would be of service to me if we could reaffirm a budget and commit to communicating before large purchases. Are you willing to do that?

After calmly and clearly stating your needs, offer space for your conversation partner to respond in a similar fashion.

Don't Let it Define You

We are targets of an incessant chatter from the media and pop culture that tells us we are defined by what we have and how much we make. Don't listen to it. Don't even hear it. Sit down in a quiet place, and think about what money means to you. Assess how you learned that. Parents? Spouse? Television show? Keep what serves you. Acknowledge what doesn't, and leave it there. Repeat annually, or even more as necessary.

Stop Diagnosing (…Unless You're a Doctor)

Mr. Rosenberg believes that "when people hear needs, it provokes compassion. When people hear diagnoses, it provokes defensiveness and attack." Often, when my wife and I are discussing a money-related issue, I find myself attempting to "solve" the situation. In my mind, I've figured out the underlying problem for both of us, and I am simply presenting what I see as the optimal solution.

What happens? She shuts down. We get nowhere. Why? Because instead of listening to what she defines as her needs, I diagnose the situation as I see it. Her voice is lost. This is, of course, incongruent with healthy discussion, and ultimately, we end up right where we started… or worse, a few steps back.

Don't diagnose the problem for another. Ask good questions. Give them the necessary space to express their needs. Then, receive the same and gently take the space your conversation partner offers to express your own needs. Continue from there.

To end, money is up there with race, religion, and politics as one of the most emotionally-charged and difficult to discuss topics. In fact, it may be the least likely topic to arise at the dinner table. As a result, we are often unable to effectively communicate about money. This can be especially true when we are put in a stressful situation with a colleague, friend, partner, spouse, parent, or child where we may have conflicting points of views heavily funneled through years of emotion. To successfully manage our own ideas of financial freedom it is imperative that we build skills, like non-violent communication, that allow us to effectively communicate about money to a multitude of important people in our lives.

Section III Summary

- Cultivate an attitude of gratitude in all things.
- Take full responsibility for all things, events, and happenstances in your life, and affirm your ability to define your future.
- Challenge scarcity-brain with new thoughts rooted in abundance.
- From this basis, communicate mindfully and non-violently about money.

Section IV

It Starts with Purpose

It all starts with purpose. What does? Well, everything, but money especially. Without purpose, we are back to the realm of mindless money. We become money zombies, mindlessly consuming, earning only to spend with no end in sight as we wander through the financial wasteland of our lives.

Sounds dramatic, does it? Good. It is dramatic. It's a waste. And little is worse than wasted potential. As we will see in the examples below, money can be used to support our freedom of time and exploration, to support our family and financial security, and as a vehicle, or conduit, that helps manifest our values and purpose in the world. In this sense, money is perhaps best understood as pure potential. So, let's not let it endlessly drip from an untended faucet.

How do we accomplish this? Well, ultimately, we must flip negative money into positive money. We must flip victimization and scarcity into their life-giving opposites. We must learn effective communication around money, both internally and externally, and remain mindful around money so as not to fall into the thralls of a force like consumption brain. But all of this comes second.

First, we must become aware of our primary purpose and start moving toward that reality. You see, your purpose is timeless, and it exists already. And when you affirm and commit to it, it pulls you forward. Challenges are confronted. Obstacles are overcome. Bad habits fall to the wayside. In this state, what doesn't serve our purpose, our grand, beautiful, effervescent vision of the future, simply fades away. You don't need it. And so, you let it go.

How do we start living a life of purpose? Let's delve into just that.

Purpose First: Intro

We are a problem-based society. Instead of thinking about what's going right, we focus on what's going wrong. What's the last positive thought you had about the direction our country is moving in? Had to think a bit, didn't you? Or worse, when's the last time you celebrated a personal accomplishment? And I mean really felt it, not just some false moment of personal congratulations. My guess is that this is also a struggle to recollect, though you could likely run off a long list of frustrations or things you would like to change about yourself.

Problem-based modalities of thinking have permeated our culture. We love to "cure" relationships. We read all about diagnosing our personal psychological ills. We are told to admit when we have a problem. Put simply, in any field or endeavor, and even our personal lives, we are taught to focus on negative aspects and from there to set about removing them so that we can finally progress.

We do this with money, as well. The general language around personal finance is fear-based. You are overspending. You aren't saving enough. You aren't investing for your future. You need more money. You don't have enough insurance. You'll never retire. You'll run out of money.

Thousands of books have been dedicated to offering solid information to cure the above ills. Hundreds of thousands of articles have been written on the topic. And yet, even as information comes more readily to our fingertips than ever, our basic behaviors haven't shifted. We still suck at personal finance.

Here's why—focusing on what's wrong does not shift behavior. At worst, we become so overwhelmed with our problems that we throw our hands in the air helplessly. At best, we engage ourselves in a brief burst of change that fizzles out just as quickly. Problem-based thinking bases our mindset in negativity. And a mindset of negativity begets further negativity.

Ultimately, attempting to become financially well without discovering and honoring the positive reasons behind this process is like putting the cart before the horse. Instead of focusing on what's wrong, we should instead focus on generating a positive and fulfilling vision of a future life.

This is the "soft" part of personal finance that very few are prepared to talk about. Purpose matters, even here... especially here.

Retirement and Financial Freedom aren't Relatable

When it comes to money we are seemingly offered only three positive visions:

- Get Rich
- Retire
- Financial Freedom (i.e. get rich *and* retire)

Unfortunately, these concepts have been hopelessly muddled by Wall Street marketing machines and, ultimately, depersonalized and distorted. Or, in some cases, they are so riddled with contrasting meanings we are left muddled and confused.

For example, the idea of "becoming rich" is an ambiguous one. What, specifically, does it mean? Does it mean owning a home? Owning a vacation home? Owning five vacation homes? The ability to buy whatever you want? A massive closet full of designer apparel? Owning ten luxury cars?

On the one hand, most of us would not mind a heavier pocketbook; however, most Americans also identify with the "middle class" and often find themselves berating wealthier individuals. Is being rich really some Beverly Hills/Laguna Beach nightmare? Would you become as weird and detached from reality as a Silicon Valley billionaire? As heartless as a Wall Street CEO? We are left confused about our feelings on the matter. Is this what having more money looks like? And, if so, do I really want to be rich?

Or how about retirement? Though sold as a vision of endless golf, the idea of retirement can seem like a slow death for those who feel they still have much to contribute in the workplace. They are not retiring *into* anything, just *away* from the present life and job. What if you like your life and job and find it gives you energy?

For others, retirement is simply too far away or not seen as a possibility. How can a thirty-year-old get inspired into financial action by a vision of retirement? It is difficult to plan for a period thirty to forty years into the future. What will you want then? Who will you be? How will your career turn out? Will you even be around?

Lastly, what does financial freedom even mean? If it signifies freedom from financial realities then most of us would be all for it. However, over the course of our adult existence most of us will confront school loans, a mortgage, unexpected health care costs, utility bills, a thousand other expenses, and, in the end, a retirement that isn't going to pay for itself. In other words, millionaire or broke, freedom from financial realities is hard to come by, if not impossible. Ultimately, "financially free" signifies we are financially unburdened, and that demands a certain amount of monetary attentiveness and savviness. The only way out is in.

In the end, the visions sold to us are little more than empty words and concepts. On the one hand, we have a hyper-charged emotional relationship with money, yet on the other hand we have no positive vision to move toward. And so, in an increasingly financialized world, the outer life of money exists in a rules-based system that will hold you accountable for your actions, yet the inner-life of money seems to run loose as if at the whims of an anarchist.

Toward Redefinitions

It is time to redefine money for ourselves. Having a purposeful relationship with money doesn't start with balancing your checkbook or defining a budget—though both these things are important. It starts with reclaiming language and evolving toward a purposeful money mindset. Money, like all things, must be *given* purpose. Rather than living our lives in pursuit of money, we should use money as a tool to serve us and how we want to live our lives.

By inverting our relationship with money so that it serves our purposes, we move from a concept of money that bristles with an unacknowledged and often negative emotional charge to one that helps us bring positivity into our lives. We must put purpose first and then use money to support that purpose.

To help us understand what that might look like, I have put together a series of categories that show purposeful expressions of money. This list is not meant to be exhaustive. There are countless ways to use money with positive purpose. Yet, broadly speaking, I believe these categories offer a strong start toward money with purpose.

The categories are as follows:

1. Money as Freedom
2. Money as Security
3. Money as a Values Conduit

As we delve into these categories, my hope is that we come out on the other end not only understanding money and our relationship to it more thoroughly, but also with an understanding of how purpose and positive intention might harness money and use it as a tool for living our best lives.

Money as Freedom I

Being financially free can mean so many different things to different people. It can be the ability to travel and stay in the finest hotels. It can be the ability to travel while carrying everything you own in a backpack. It can be living in a penthouse in Manhattan after being made partner at your law firm. Or, it can be living debt-free in a "tiny home" out in the sticks. Driving a Tesla or riding your bike, starting a new business or retiring early, focusing on your passions or focusing on your family, buying an organic farm or simply affording organic at the local co-op—these can all be forms of financial freedom.

To be clear, in its truest form, financial freedom signifies the ability to live off your investments without having to worry about a job or running out of money. It is a work-optional time-period. You *may* work because you love what you do or you enjoy certain projects. Or, you may *not* work because you'd rather be sitting on a beach in Costa Rica.

However, ending the conversation at this base definition robs us of an opportunity to create a personalized financial freedom that is reflective of our own hopes, goals, opportunities, *and* realities. When we truly assess our own vision of financial freedom, we explore varied and deeply personal territory.

You see, the problem with the idea of financial freedom isn't that it is an unattainable ideal, it's that we often idealize the unattainable. When we see photoshopped images of financial success presented by the media and various celebrities, it's all too easy to confuse true financial freedom with these unattainable standards. If you follow this path, whatever financial freedom you end up with, if any, will be the result of someone else's dream—not your own.

For example, we often imagine that the path to financial freedom necessarily means more money. Think of all the time we spend daydreaming about winning the lottery. However, according to the National Endowment for Financial Education, 70% of people who receive a large amount of money or financial "windfall" will see it dwindle away within a few short years (Chan 2016). In fact, some lottery winners have gone bankrupt after winning millions of dollars. As you can see, the short-term ability to consume more may lead to *less* financial freedom in the end. Unfortunately, a similar story plays out for many professional athletes after their playing days are over. Obviously, there is more to financial freedom than simply having more money.

That isn't to say that financial freedom has nothing to do with money. Of course it does. It's just not about the endless pursuit of it. Often, the more we make, the more we spend, because more money often means more things—a bigger house, a nicer car, or a larger lifestyle.

Notably, we see this same dynamic with overeating. One study of moviegoers gave different bags of popcorn to different individuals entering the theater (Wansink and Junyong 2005). The individuals in groups one and two received either a medium bag of fresh popcorn or a large bag of fresh popcorn. Similarly, groups three and four also received either a medium or a large bag though there was one rather large difference. You see, groups three and four received horribly stale popcorn. Like really stale. Fourteen days old in fact.

What did the researchers find? The study found that groups two and four ate significantly more popcorn simply because their carton was larger. Indeed, people ate more of that stale, fourteen-day-old popcorn simply because it was there! In other words, palatable or not, the more food that is on our plate, the more soda in the carton, or the more chips in the bag, the more we will likely eat.

If you have ever heard someone say, "That cash is burning a hole in my pocket," you know that a similar dynamic plays out in our financial lives. We often buy things simply because we have the capacity to do so, not because of any need or, at times, even want.

In the popcorn study, participants reported that they were personally unaffected by the larger portions despite data showing otherwise (Lang 2005). It's like that with money. We don't even know how we are behaving, money zombies through-and-through, until we are jolted awake by financial realities.

Mindless though it may be, the problem with the endless pursuit of more is that it never ends. Financial freedom, in contrast, is about the pursuit of enough. And each of us needs to ask ourselves, realistically: What does "enough" mean to me?

In asking this question, we close our ears to the cultural siren song that measures us by our relative consumption, and instead, we begin to hear what our unique and soulful contributions to life might be—this includes our work and its financial reward, but also such things as art, love, kindness, service, family, community, and passion projects.

Financial freedom has more to do with our lifestyle than our income level. If we are pursuing a passion, financial freedom is the ability to do so without excessively worrying about rent or debt payments. If we are starting a new business, it is the ability to stay afloat and focused during the initial growth stage. If we are looking for more time in a day, it is the ability to unburden ourselves of time-consuming and unwanted tasks and distractions by paying someone else to do them. It may even be as simple as developing more mindful and intentional spending habits that gradually liberate us from consumption brain. No matter how it finds expression, what matters is what financial freedom means to you.

I don't mean to imply that any of this will be easy—it will take a great deal of dedication, habit-building, and, possibly, some mental and emotional shifts. However, it is important that we realize that, for many of us, financial freedom is possible without a huge increase in income or a financial windfall. In other words, it's not an "if/then" equation (i.e. if I made "X" amount of money then I would feel financially free). Rather, it's something we can start reflecting upon and working toward today regardless of our starting point.

Money as Freedom II: Time isn't Money; Money is Time

Even more than money, one of the most precious things we spend in our lives is time. Most of us barter time for money. More money, in many cases, demands more time. This can be as simple as having to come into the office a couple of Saturdays a month or being available by email after traditional work hours. It can also mean taking on another job or project to earn a little extra income.

In many cases putting more time in for financial gain is worth it. However, the question we need to ask ourselves is whether we are working to preserve a certain lifestyle—like working sixty-hour weeks and not seeing your kids just to afford that big, beautiful house you don't even spend much time in. Or, like putting every cent you earn into presenting a certain image—the clothes you wear, the car you drive, your loft apartment—but precariously living paycheck to paycheck with little in savings. Are these actions the financial equivalent of running in place? Or is the time we are putting in an investment in a better or more sustainable financial future?

In this sense, our time buys our money. Thankfully, however, that's a two-way street, and, ultimately, our money can buy time. In fact, beyond a certain level of sustenance and financial security, time might be the most important resource that money can buy.

At the end of the day, you're not saving for money's sake. You're saving for something else—time with your kids or grandkids, time to sail the world, time without distractions, or maybe just time to be free of financial anxiety. In other words, your savings and your investment portfolio have a function, and the purpose of seeing "money as time," in contrast to "time as money," is to personalize that function.

Many individuals and families who aggressively save a large portion of their income and limit their debt usage have "bought" the opportunity for a sabbatical, an early retirement, or, simply, a more financially secure retirement. Any way you look at it, these are ultimately investments in time free of financial stress. Similarly, when a couple decides that one parent should be a stay-at-home mom or dad, they, as a couple, are investing in time with their kid(s).

It is easy to fall into the trap of thinking of our savings as some vague collection of financial assets. However, a more complete picture shows that they are investments in our financial freedom, future entrepreneurial endeavors, the ability to do more service-oriented work, or simply time. In this sense, money becomes a positive catalyst for unlocking our dreams and goals, rather than just another facet of life that stresses us out. You aren't saving to amass a fortune for no reason; you are saving to amass a fortunate life full of time well spent.

For us as individuals, time is a limited resource, and we simply do not have the ability to know how much we ultimately have. To that end, it is crucial that we spend every moment mindfully, while also being conscious of how we can save up for even greater future allocations of this most precious resource.

To end, time isn't money, money is time. And what's time? You guessed it: freedom.

Money as Freedom III: Optionality

Interlaced with the ideas of money as freedom and time is something less heady, and perhaps more easily understood and relatable. Money can be used to expand the choices available to us. Indeed, money *is* optionality.

If you have five dollars in your pocket for dinner, there are only so many restaurants available to you. Make that twenty dollars, and you won't struggle to find a good meal. And, if you're careful about where you go, you could probably pick up the tab for a friend as well!

In other words, a little extra cash may result in a nicer, or even a larger, dinner, but most importantly, it results in a wider array of options from which to choose.

On a larger scale, someday you might decide that you cannot bear another day at your job. So, you go home, and you talk it over with your spouse. You express your frustration, maybe you cry a little bit. Your spouse does an incredible job listening and empathizing with you, and you feel supported. But then, the moment comes to discuss realities. Like many families today, you are living paycheck to paycheck. You don't have anything saved, and your school loans aren't going to pay themselves. Your partner knows this, and you know this.

Frustrating? Of course. But it's also reality. Most of us do not have the option of leaving our job without another opportunity lined up, complete with adequate pay and full benefits.

Now, imagine this scenario. You finish expressing your frustration, and your spouse looks at you and says, "Well, you know we just finished paying off our loans which means our monthly fixed expenses are way down and our rainy day fund is at $50,000. Plus, I'm loving my job and feel very secure in my position there right now. How would you feel about quitting now, taking a month or two off to rejuvenate yourself, and then start looking for a job you love?"

It is plain to see that money offers us options. Paying off your last cent of debt gives you options. Increasing your annual income by $25,000 gives you options. Having a war chest of savings for a time of need opens worlds of opportunity that are closed off to others.

There are countless ways to manifest this choice. If you're on a set salary, get creative about reducing expenses to see what you can save every month. Believe it or not, many people find a lot of joy in this process. Or, pick up a side gig and save 100% of your income from that second job or use it to aggressively pay down debt. Many couples find that when they both work outside the home they can comfortably live off only one spouse's income. This allows them to allocate all of the second income to long-term savings and investments.

As an example, let's say your income is sufficient for household expenses, and your spouse's monthly paycheck, after taxes and benefits, is $3,000. Saving just $2,000 of that paycheck each month and investing it at a conservative 5.0% rate of return compounded annually would net you over $300,000 in ten years.

What could you do with an extra $300,000 in long-term savings? Would it take some pressure off your sense of job security? Would it free you up to support your kids through college? Could you take a sabbatical or start thinking about retiring early or starting your own business?

Regardless of what you would do, notice that what you really have are choices. That extra $300,000 represents the ability to explore options. Money is a way to express our freedom and maximize the choices available to us.

Reflection Questions on Money as Freedom

1. If you *felt* financially free, how would your life be different? What would you do?

2. What does "enough" look like for you?

3. If you reimagined money as time (i.e., allowing you the opportunity to choose how to spend your time) how would it change the way you think about savings and/or your investment portfolio? Would you save more aggressively to invest in time or your vision of financial freedom? Would it make you consider how you truly want to be spending your time and how you can use your present and future resources to get there? Would it change anything else in your life?

4. How could you reduce your spending or increase your income to create more optionality in your life? What would that look like for you? What would it feel like?

Money as Security I

Recently, I had dinner with a client of mine, let's call her Jan, and she told me of the money habits of a former romantic partner. "To him, money was like a scourge," she said. "He couldn't rid himself of it fast enough. As a result, he would spend, almost immediately, every cent he made."

Of course, this meant they never had adequate savings, not even some rainy day cash to help them transition without undue monetary stress (whether the transition came out of personal desire or was necessitated by unexpected life events).

But Jan felt differently about money. She went on. "I always liked having money. I was good with it, and it gave me comfort to know I had a fallback plan if difficulties arose for me or a loved one."

What Jan was tapping into were the positive feelings that come from using money to help secure what's important and meaningful in our lives. This is our second category of using money with purpose: Money as Security.

Change is unavoidable. It is not to be feared, but expected. And it's important to note that all the money in the world cannot prepare you for or comfort you during the many life-altering events that will likely confront you over the years. Receiving word of a loved one's cancer diagnosis, or any other serious disease or injury, cannot be glossed over with a trip to the mall and a new watch. Rather, we must face these difficulties with love, patience, empathy, steadfastness, and resilience.

However, those who understand how money can be a source of healthy security and who do the necessary tasks like starting a monthly savings plan and buying adequate insurance will, in many cases, have dissolved the added stress of financial worry during difficult times.

Injury, illness, accidents, emergencies, losing a job—all come with financial realities and consequences that must be confronted. In the moment, people rise to the occasion to provide heroic amounts of service and comfort. But the long-term effects of these hardships can be felt just as intensely in your pocketbook.

A loved one's battle with cancer, for instance, can force you to tap into your job's 401(k) plan. Now, not only are your savings depleted by unexpected medical bills and the loss of your partner's income, but the retirement you saw happening in ten years has now been pushed back indefinitely. A child's illness can force a parent to put career ambitions on hold to stay home for a few years. Similarly, and more positively, a surprise pregnancy can come with surprise bills for the unprepared.

Here we see again that personal finance doesn't start with money, savings, or investments. It starts with keeping the end in mind. You don't put money in a rainy day fund because it's always fun to save. You build the rainy day fund because you know that sometimes it doesn't just rain, it pours. And, whether or not those storm clouds ever arrive, you feel secure that you have a hearty umbrella in hand should you require it. In this sense, money as security is a healthy thing to strive for and a purpose worth devoting time and resources toward.

Most of us have someone in our family who has something akin to "Depression-mentality." That is, the tendency of individuals who lived through The Great Depression to horde cash because they've experienced what extreme financial insecurity feels like due to the dire circumstances of the period. Often, we see this mentality as a negative, and at its extremes it can certainly keep individuals from enjoying life. However, there is wisdom here and certainly a lesson for all of us to consider.

Without imploring you to horde money under your mattress and in your walls, viewing money as security and diligently working toward that security (via smart saving, investment, and spending habits as well as seeking opportunities to increase your earnings) is an extremely positive thing. In other words, *feeling* financially secure is something worth working toward and can offer a grand sense of purpose. Similarly, *being* financially secure can free us up in so many other ways—mentally, emotionally, and, as we saw above, it allows for greater opportunity to explore the options in front of us.

Money as Security II

I have a good friend who is attempting to design and market a transportable tiny home, complete with a hydroponic plant garden, a water purifier, and a chicken coop, for less than $10,000. Once moved into, his hope is that an individual's basic needs will be met—food, shelter, water—regardless of what happens in the job market or broader economy. After I listened to his plans, we talked excitedly about the incredible creativity that could be unleashed if people pursued their art or passion untethered to a traditional idea of a daily income, with all its stresses and demands.

My friend's plans for a tiny home got me thinking. Security doesn't have to mean a pension, a million-dollar investment portfolio, and fully paying down your $500,000 mortgage (though it certainly can, and each of these sound great to me). It can simply mean parking your $10,000 tiny home on a small parcel of land and spending your days caring for your garden. It's certainly attractive to imagine pursuing your passions, interests, and service opportunities without the immediate need for money because you have a roof over your head and food in your belly.

Extreme? Maybe. Simple? Absolutely. An example of purposeful money? Without a doubt.

When I discuss life insurance with my financial planning clients, I don't start with, "You need to purchase life insurance." It wouldn't be productive. Instead, the conversation starts with "What's important to you?"

For many families, the answer is "If I pass away, I want to make sure my spouse or partner doesn't have to work outside the home while raising our children." Others want to ensure their children's college expenses are paid for. Still others want to give to a charity they care about. All to say, once they declare what is most meaningful to them, their monthly life insurance premiums shift from a burdensome obligation to something they feel grateful for the ability to afford.

This is a mental shift we need to make with all financial basics (e.g. retirement savings, rainy day fund, spending plans, other insurance products, etc.). None of these are compulsory pains in the neck, mandated by some ill-meaning financial system. We opt into confronting the financial basics because they tangibly support what is meaningful to us.

Seeing money for the security and balance it can offer in extreme situations is a perfect example of how we can use money with purpose. Not only is the desire for a sense of financial security a normal goal, it is something we can hold close to help drive our everyday financial decisions.

Reflection Questions on Money as Security

1. What would it mean to you to feel financially secure? Why is that important for you? What does that look like?

2. What steps could you implement today to help you achieve that sense of security?

3. Imagine it's three years in the future, and you are feeling incredibly financially secure. As you look back on the previous three years, how did you go about executing or creating more financial security in your life?

Money as a Values Conduit I

At its core, the monetary system is a system of integrity (Kinder, *The Seven Stages of Money Maturity* 1999). It is value-based, meaning this is how we value each other's services and goods, but is also a process by which we affirm our own values. It would be overly burdensome for the farmer to barter his corn for meat, fruit, clothes, a house, entertainment, etc. Instead, he sells his corn for dollars and uses the money to purchase both everyday necessities and affordable wants. Selling his corn at the market for a fair price, he feels valued for his work. Using his hard-earned money to purchase clothes for his kids he affirms that he values the welfare of his children.

Your financial decisions, both in the receipt and spending of money, should honor your core values. It is in this way that we express our inner wholeness. However, all too often our inner life is compartmentalized. We might value time with our family above all else, but maybe we were taught from a young age, explicitly and implicitly, that providing for our family is our highest purpose. Now, it is honorable to provide for one's family, but when done at the expense of our core values, in this case time with family, we do ourselves and our family an extreme disservice.

One of my core values is creative expression. Acknowledging that truth and honoring it led me to using my money to record two albums as a singer-songwriter. I remember both instances with incredible joy and gratitude. I should note that both albums were expensive endeavors for someone in their twenties (which I was at the time). But to honor my value and aspirations, I saved up the necessary financial resources and used them with intentionality from start to finish.

I should also note that neither album sold particularly well, or really at all. But selling my music wasn't what I valued. Creating music was what I found fulfilling, regardless of how it sold. This is not meant as a judgment on professional artists who do sell their work. It is simply to say that this activity was about my own personal evolution, and as such I was willing to spend money on the endeavor. The point is to acknowledge and honor what it is you value and find ways to ensure that your financial decisions, both grand and mundane, are reflective of what you hold dear at your core.

When we start with purpose, we can also see money as a values conduit that passes along our emotional spectrum—expressing gratitude, appreciation, affirmation, and love—as well as reflecting our personal values in real time.

Money contains emotional energy whether we like it or not. With every purchase, you are saying, "I value this," whether it is the efforts of another, their service, or their product. Similarly, when you sell your time or services for wages or compensation, you too are saying, "I value my time and this work at this price."

Of course, this basic reality mostly goes unacknowledged on a day-to-day basis. We may consider it when evaluating a large purchase or when changing jobs, but for the most part our daily exchanges of money slip beneath our radar. However, despite the lack of attention, our earning and spending is still charged with emotional energy. It simply can't be avoided.

This lack of awareness can be dangerous. It's crucial to always be mindful of our core values, especially around money. From this basis, we can pause before a financial transaction and ask ourselves if it honors our values.

For example, my wife spent a great deal of time living and working in Africa, and it was important to her when we got engaged that we did not add to demand for diamonds mined unethically in countries like the Democratic Republic of Congo. Instead, we found a vintage wedding ring online that we loved and was much cheaper than a new ring. In this case, our values were clear. We valued our relationship, our ability to communicate, and our commitment—not the size of a diamond. Moreover, we valued safe and ethical working conditions, something we felt couldn't be guaranteed with a new product.

Similar examples can be found in opting to shop at your local co-op or farmer's market, joining a CSA, choosing to ignore the environmentally detrimental "fast-fashion" industry and instead buying ethically-made and long-lasting clothing items, or supporting local businesses over big-box competitors.

Of course, not everything is black and white, and we are often faced with deciding between different shades of grey with our money decisions. In these scenarios, we simply must make the best decision we can and move on with our lives. However, by honoring and assessing our values throughout the decision-making process, or, put simply, giving our values a seat at the table, we can make decisions that reflect and move us toward our purpose.

Money as a Values Conduit II: Charitable Giving

A great example of how we transfer and affirm our values with money is found in our charitable contributions. When we assess our financial reality through a lens of gratitude and abundance and see that there is room for charitable giving, these positive values become attached to the money throughout the exchange. In this way, when we give, we make our values concrete, manifesting them in real dollars and cents.

With charitable giving, we once again see the end in the beginning. With the dollars we contribute, we see a young child being fed nourishing food. We see a family obtaining shelter. We see a young woman receiving a college scholarship. Of course, these results are not solely due to money. They also involve people donating time and effort for the welfare of others. However, the movement of money throughout our society can do immense good.

Charitable, or conscious giving can be so many things. When I was in high school, my mom underwent treatment for breast cancer. Kind friends and neighbors brought over countless meals for us during that time. It was not that we couldn't afford food. We could. But it was one less thing to worry about, and it gave us the gift of time and community. I'm forever grateful to those generous people and families.

When we consciously make room for charitable contributions, we are infusing money with one of our highest human purposes, service to another. We're saying, "I'm grateful to have these financial resources, and I am grateful to share them with you." In other words, we have honored the importance of money and what it can do, as well as our efforts and intentions. Then, with a heart full of gratitude, we pass on money to someone who can do great good with it.

Charitable giving can be done on a grand scale, like a multi-millionaire philanthropist creating her own foundation, but it can also be done on a small, or more personalized scale. For example, giving ten dollars per month to an organization that provides breakfasts at school to underprivileged children can go an incredibly long way.

The person on the receiving side of a charitable exchange can also enter with a healthy mindset. This person can say, "I'm grateful that you are willing to share your financial resources so we may put them to positive use in our community." The individual does not receive with the resentful or suspicious mindset of… "Well, she's filthy rich and has money to spare," or, "They could give much more than they do."

Instead, a healthy recipient confidently honors the giving heart of another as well as the good that money can do in the world. When we dismiss the donor, we dismiss the importance of the gift. There is extreme virtue in the act of giving regardless of the amount, especially so when sacrifice is involved.

In *Wherever You Go, There You Are,* Jon Kabat-Zinn writes, "At its deepest level, there is no giver, no gift, and no recipient… only the universe rearranging itself." (Kabat-Zinn 2005)

Ultimately, charitable giving is one of the most relatable forms of connecting purpose with money, as we feel compelled by who we are and what we value to allocate our financial resources toward the betterment of our world.

Money as a Values Conduit III: Supporting Family & Loved Ones

During the process of writing this book, my wife shared some incredible news with me. I was going to be a father. As any parent knows, "elated" doesn't describe the well of emotion that arises at such a time. I was overjoyed and filled to the brim with love. I was so excited to be on this journey with my wife, and I simply couldn't wait to meet our little one.

However, I felt other emotions as well. For example, at times I felt scared and slightly overwhelmed—especially by financial realities. You see, I had just left a steady paycheck to start my own business, and though I was enjoying every second of entrepreneurship, I now had an added pressure to succeed.

Before I left my job, my wife and I felt like we should be able to make it roughly two years before I needed to start making a decent income. This would take some pressure off me and allow me to focus on building my business without being overly stressed about the immediate bottom line. But here I was, not even fully "live" with the new business, and we were finding out that our family was about to expand. My timeline for needing to be profitable at my new firm had been moved up.

It was at this moment that I learned the fullness of how providing for one's family can fill an individual with financial purpose. I had heard my dad share similar stories. One, particularly poignant for me, is that after starting his own business soon after I was born, he was only months away from losing the house to the bank. With a wife and two young kids to provide for, he burned the midnight oil to bring in the necessary funds to get back on track and ultimately made it through. My brother-in-law also confessed to me that everything changed for him after his first child was born. He felt less career angst and simply felt grateful that he had a job that helped support his young family.

I appreciated these sentiments in theory, but I wasn't prepared for the reality of the feeling. My idea of success had shifted from mostly intangibles, like a desire to help people live lives of meaning and purpose, to include something very tangible: to earn enough income to provide for my growing family.

Overnight, everything changed. It didn't matter that I was introverted and was hoping to slowly build my network over a period of years. I needed to start growing my network today so I could meet potential clients who were looking for the expertise and service I could provide.

In other words, my purpose, or my "why" for growing my business and my income had now superseded all obstacles. No more procrastination. No more "I'll make that phone call tomorrow." I go to that event, I send that email, and I make that phone call because of my child.

And here's what I'm getting at. When it comes to supporting your family and friends, whether it's putting food on the table, helping with education costs, or providing for an elderly parent, using money for this purpose is always an act of love. And if the welfare of others is a core "why" for your overall financial life plan, you can know that it is an honorable one.

Do you have a loved one who inspires you to action or for whom you feel called to provide financial support on some level? Maybe it's your spouse or your children, a niece or nephew, or even your own parents. Or, maybe you are young and a recipient of financial support from your own parents or another loved one. For example, it has become common for adult children to move back in with their parents after college to save on rent while paying down school loans or pursuing, say, an unpaid internship.

Often, we provide and receive this support within some broader routine without considering its deeper implications. In this way, we stay firmly within the mundane. However, money with purpose teaches us to work backward. First, we assess our "why" and then move to "what" and "how."

When it comes to supporting your family, the activity, I suspect, is done out of love. Sure, there might be some obligation involved, but that obligation only exists *because* of love. Whether you are giving or receiving, bring the financial support back from dollars and cents to the reason you are doing it in the first place—love—and be grateful for it.

Reflection Questions on Money as a Values Conduit

1. If an anthropologist took a deep dive into your purchase decisions for the last year, what would he deem you value?

2. How could you connect your values more fully with your spending? What would that look like?

3. If you relate to the idea of giving more, how might you give more proactively in your life? Who or what would you give to?

4. How do your finances help you support that which you value most, like your personal well-being, your passions, and your loved ones?

Core Values

A client recently expressed to me that she aches to travel, to be able to hop in her car and go where she wills without feeling like her financial and life obligations are holding her back.

Freedom. She *aches* for freedom. She *values* freedom.

What is dearest to you? What do you hold at the core of you? What are your deepest held values?

If you're having trouble thinking of what your values might be, here's a thought experiment. What upsets you more than anything? What are your pet peeves? For me, when I am stuck in traffic and someone slides out and starts driving on the shoulder, only to cut back in a mile down the line, it drives me batty. Why?

When I really think about it, what bothers me most is that these individuals, in my mind, are acting selfishly. They are not thinking of others, only themselves and their immediate needs. So, is my core value "not being selfish"? No, not quite. But what would its positive opposite look like? Empathy and understanding come to mind. As a result, it becomes apparent to me that I value empathy a great deal.

Here's where it gets interesting. As I started to understand empathy as a core value of mine, more values revealed themselves. Thinking deeper about my appreciation for empathy, I realized that I also really appreciate deep listening. Very little makes me feel more respected than when someone really, truly listens to me.

Ultimately, my root desire for empathy and understanding also leads me to value skillful and honest listening. Before I fully understood this, I was mostly doing back office work at an investment firm. I rarely communicated with clients or even co-workers. In many respects, I was siloed off.

For years, I thought this was best for me. I have an introverted personality, and for my entire life people had told me that I'm shy, an assessment I had come to believe as fact. Given this belief, of course I didn't want to be client-facing! I wasn't supposed to want to talk to people. But as I started to understand what I value, I realized that by serving clients as a financial life planner, as a coach, as a guide, and as a *listener,* I had the opportunity to align my career with some of my deepest held values. In other words, I had moved from values to purpose and then allowed my purpose to align my life with what I find most fulfilling.

If you're lost in the weeds at this point, let's stop and try to create a list of the values that you hold dear. In the end, shoot for three to five. The point is not to be exhaustive, but simply to hone in on what is core to you. Feel free to take five minutes or so to meditate and think about what these values really are. Below are some prompts to help you in this process.

1. If you had to give a speech on three values and why they are the most important, what would they be and why?

2. In the example above, my client ached to be able to travel on a whim without restrictions for work or family. She valued her personal freedom. What do you ache for? In moments of self-reflection, what do you long for? What does this say about your values?

3. We can also come to know our values by assessing what we don't value and looking for its opposite. What are your pet peeves? What type of behavior or activity frustrates you to no end? Now, instead of focusing on that, focus instead on its opposite. Is this one of your values?

Now, write your values down and start carrying them with you on a small piece of paper or in a notebook wherever you go. Maybe the list doesn't feel spot-on yet. That's fine. Use what you have, but let the broader questions sit under the surface. *What are my core values? How do I honor them?*

What's Your Why?

Now that we have a working list of values, let's ask an even more basic set of questions.

What gets you up in the morning? What compels you to leave the comfort of your warm sheets and engage in the necessary tasks of life? What gets you back on your feet when you get knocked down? What fills you with passion? Or love?

What's your "why"?

Your "why" is like oxygen for the lungs. When you breathe it in purely, intentionally, it fills you with focus and calm. It is the blood in your veins… your base element… the stuff of life.

Take your list of core values. Thinking broadly, how do you honor them? What strand of life connects them within you? What spirit flows throw them?

In my experience, most "whys" concern family or some sort of religiosity or spirituality. Some are focused on creativity or an empathetic purpose. You might even have greater and lesser "whys," or you may notice that your "why" has shifted over time. It's okay. All are welcomed here. All are accepted.

Maybe your "why" is to be connected to the universal flow and to live a life full of love and laughter with friends, family, and loved ones. Or maybe your "why" is to offer your young children a stable and loving home. It might also be to honor the well of creativity within you by soulfully expressing your creative impulses via your work.

Your "why" can be more tangible or personal, as well. If you work in sales or marketing, your "why" might be "connect people with services and products that simplify their lives and allow them to focus on what matters to them." An individual in public health may be inspired to heal a thousand individuals through healing the health care system. A grandfather's "why" might be the opportunity to spend as much time as possible with his grandchildren.

And so, I ask again, "What's your 'why'?"

A few prompts might help you hone in on this. Imagine you won the lottery. Jackpot! You are now a multi-millionaire. Or, maybe a rich aunt left you with a massive inheritance no one knew she had. Either way, all your present and future financial needs are more than taken care of. Once the shock subsides and the money hits your bank account, you sit down at your favorite coffee shop with some serious questions on your mind. How will you live your life? Are you going to change anything? What will you do with your time?

What would you do? Would you leave your job? Would you change careers? Would you move to a different town? How would you allocate your time? Would you spend more of it with your family? Or, maybe you'd spend more time traveling, like sailing down the coast in your new sailboat.

Seriously, what would you do? Unleash your creativity. Allow yourself to dream!

Now, look at things from another direction. Stephen Covey, in *The 7 Habits of Highly Effective People*, prompts us to consider we are watching our funeral from above (Covey 2013). Who is there? What kind of people are they? What do they think of you? How would they describe you?

Similarly, George Kinder, in his book *Life Planning for You: How to Design and Deliver the Life of Your*

Dreams, asks us to consider how we might feel if we just found out we only have one day left to live. What are our regrets? What did we miss out on? Who did we not get to be? (Kinder and Rowland, *Life Planning For You: How to Design and Deliver the Life of Your Dreams,* 2014)

When I first confronted this question, prompted by a loving friend and mentor, tears rolled down my cheeks. My wife. I didn't get to spend enough time with my wife. She is, you see, at the core of me. I also realized that I had never allowed myself to fulfill my creative ambitions. I had songs I'd never played for anyone. Albums of music I'd never given away, let alone sold. And I had countless books that I had to begin writing. I realized that if I didn't start writing, daily, with a purpose to create, that I would age to become a bitter individual full of regret. Writing. Creating. These, too, are parts of my "why."

How would you like to be remembered? If your life continued as is, would you have regrets? What would it look like to engage in what fulfills you?

What's your "why"?

Take a day. Take a week. But spend time on this question. If you know exactly what your "why" is, good for you. Keep going. If this question scares the living daylights out of you, that's great too. Fear is a wonderful sign that we are onto something. Breathe into it. Engage it. Listen to yourself. Learn from your thoughts and feelings. Engage with what is at your core.

Becoming Poetically Whole

Like the Anticipatory Principle discussed in Section I, there is another principle of appreciative inquiry called the Poetic Principle. The Poetic Principle states that human organizations, and humans themselves, are more like a constantly evolving book than a machine. In their book, *Appreciative Inquiry: A Positive Revolution in Change*, David Cooperrider and Diana Whitney write, "Pasts, presents, and futures are endless sources of learning, inspiration, and interpretation, like the endless interpretive possibilities in a poem or a literary text." (Cooperrider and Whitney 2005)

In any given moment of our life, we are offered the opportunity to redefine our experience of the past, present, and future. Though we often feel propelled by the past and its rigid lessons, we can let go of our personal narratives with a turn of the page. Then, putting pen to paper, we allow a new framing of the past or present, or even the compelling pull of a future yet to be experienced, to write into existence a more fulfilling and positive path forward. Like poets turning a phrase or songwriters seeking a greater rhythm, we too can add lines to our lives that we never imagined before.

Manifesting Purpose

Here's how to manifest purpose in your own life. We start with our core values, as these help us define who we are and what is important to us. Then, from our values, we mix together a sense of purpose, a deep and vibrant "why" to our lives. However, it doesn't end there.

Next, we must provide direction and a sense of movement to our purpose. How are you manifesting and realizing your "why" over time? How do you bring it more fully to life?

We do this by creating a positive vision of our future life, and then we begin moving toward that vision with intention. If the values are the boat, your purpose is the rudder, and the horizon beyond is your vision. But the sail that catches the wind to bring you across ocean and sea, that is intention.

Here's the trick. The positive vision that pulls you forward should be able to be realized within the next one to two years. It's okay to have an overarching vision, one that would emerge over a period of decades, or a lifetime. However, for most people it is difficult to keep such a long-term vision in the forefront of their minds daily. Instead, break down the long-term vision into shorter-term milestones. If you'd like to be known as a successful author with multiple books to your name when you are sixty, set an intention to write 250 words per day for the next year. If you'd like to be a NCAA Division I head basketball coach in fifteen years, set an intention to get an assistant coaching job within two years.

Get clear on your core values. Know your "why." And then ask yourself: What's my vision? How do I live with purpose? How do I act with intention?

And when the answer arrives, let that guide you to shore.

Purposeful Money

We know that when it comes to money most of us lack purpose. But now we know how to start moving forward. Within us, we feel a positive impulse beginning to emanate outward. This is what happens when we know our values—our "why" becomes self-evident. And from our "why," vision, purpose, and intention become manifest in our lives.

As a result, we begin, constantly and intuitively, asking two questions about our personal finances:

1. How do my financial decisions reflect my core values?
2. How can my financial resources, present and future, help me move toward my envisioned life?

The answer, ultimately, is yours. In fact, your answer is the only one that matters. No one knows you like you do. No one cares about your core values as much as you do. No one knows how to honor them as you do.

Here is the thing about vision. No one will ever help you execute your vision until you declare it aloud. Softly at first, we whisper it to ourselves, to a trusted friend, loved one, or advisor. But, like a river overflowing, we progress from creative spark to excited whisper, from an urge softly spoken to an ache declared into existence.

Jim Rohn said something similar once. "If you don't design your own life plan, chances are you'll fall into someone else's plan. And guess what they have planned for you? Not much."

So, what's your life plan?

Final Thoughts

Some books seek to give you step-by-step guidelines to become a millionaire. This book does not presume that being a millionaire is a goal of yours. In fact, this book would argue that becoming a millionaire is not a goal at all. Rather, it may be a by-product of purposeful living, or a means to a more meaningful end.

All to say, who you are, what you are about, your goals, purpose, fulfillment… these are what matter, and they help us create the signposts of our financial life.

Money is not an end in and of itself, nor is it a beginning. It's a means to an end, an entity we can use to transfer value, fulfill our needs, live our values, and move further into a life of purpose.

As you reflect on this book, do not forget the core message—purpose is everything. When we live with purpose we live more meaningful and satisfying lives. Our financial lives are simply an aspect of our overall well-being, not to be segmented or compartmentalized. There is not one set of values acceptable around money and business and another acceptable in life. Bringing purpose from the pew to our daily transactions and rituals all the way to our long-term savings and planning can help us live meaningful lives.

Bibliography

American Psychological Association. 2015. Stress in America: Paying with Our Health. Survey, American Psychological Association .

American Psychological Association. 2015. Stress in America: Paying With Our Health. Survey, Washington, D.C.: American Psychological Association.

Bryan, Mark, and Julia Cameron . 1999. *Money Drunk, Money Sober; 90 Days to Financial Freedom.* New York City: Wellspring/Ballantine.

Chan, Melissa. 2016. *Here's How Winning the Lottery Makes You Miserable* . January 12. Accessed June 12, 2018. http://time.com/4176128/powerball-jack-pot-lottery-winners/.

Christopher J. Boyce, Gordon D.A. Brown, and Simon C. Moore. 2010. "Money and Happiness: Rank of Income, Not Income, Affects Life Satisfaction." *Psychological Science* 21 (4): 471-475.

Cooperrider, David L., and Diana Whitney. 2005. *Appreciative Inquiry: A Positive Revolution in Change* . San Francisco: Berrett-Koehler Publishers, Inc.

Covey, Stephen R. 2013. *The 7 Habits of HIghly Successful People* . New York City : RosettaBooks .

Gabler, Neal. 2016. "The Secret-Shame of Middle Class Americans ." *The Atlantic* , May .

Kabat-Zinn, Jon. 2005. Wherever You Go, There You Are: Mindfulness Meditation in Everyday Life. New York City : Hachette Books .

Kinder, George. 1999. *The Seven Stages of Money Maturity.* New York : Delacorte Press.

Kinder, George, and Mary Rowland. 2014. *Life Planning For You: How to Design and Deliver the Life of Your Dreams.* Littleton, MA: Serenity Point Press.

Lang, Susan S. 2005. *Bad Popcorn in Big Buckets.* November 9. Accessed July 11, 2018. http://news.cornell.edu/stories/2005/11/big-portions-influence-overeating-much-taste-even-when-food-tastes-lousy-cornell.

Mischel, W. , Shoda, Y., Rodriguez, MI. 1989. "Delay of Gratification in Children ." *Science* 244 (4907): 933-938.

Papp, Lauren M. , E. Mark Cummings , and Marcie C. Goeke-Morey. 2009. "For Richer, For Poorer: Money as a Topic of Marital Conflict in the Home." *Family Relations: Interdisciplinary Journal of Applied Family Studies* (58): 91-103.

Rampell, Catherine. 2009. *Money Fights Predict Divorce Rates.* December 7. Accessed September 9, 2017. https://economix.blogs.nytimes.com/2009/12/07/money-fights-predict-divorce-rates/.

Rosenberg, Marshall B. 2015. *Non-Violent Communication: A Language of life .* 3rd. Puddle Dancer Press .

The Board of Governors of the Federal Reserve System . 2018 . *Report on Economic Well-Being of U.S. Households in 2017 .* Report , Washington, D.C.: The Board of Governors of the Federal Reserve System .

The Center for Appreciative Inquiry . 2016. *Principles of Appreciative Inquiry .* Accessed May 24, 2018. https://www.centerforappreciativeinquiry.net/more-on-ai/principles-of-appreciative-inquiry/.

Wagner, Richard B. 2017. *Interior Finance .* January 8. Accessed June 12, 2018. https://www.worthliving.com/2003/01/interior-finance/.

Wansink, Brian, and Kim Junyong. 2005. "Bad Popcorn in Big Buckets: Portion Size Can Influence Intake as Much as Taste." *Journal of Nutrition Education and Behavior* 37 (5): 242–245.

Acknowledgments

First and foremost, I must acknowledge the incredible work that my writing coach and editor, James Samimi-Farr, did on this book. He took what must have felt like a jumble of words and ideas and helped me shape it into a focused manuscript. More, he kept me focused and writing during a time that saw me start my own business and witness the birth of my first child.

Thank you to the team at Calumet Editions, who brought this book from a Microsoft Word document to the professional product you see in front of you. Gary, Ian, and the rest of the team took my authorial ambitions seriously from day one, and for that I will forever be grateful.

To my dad, who was and is the rare type to talk about personal finance at the dinner table, thank you for teaching me the importance of money by framing it within all the things in life that matter more. To my sister and business partner, Courtney Ranstrom, who grounds our practice when my head is in the clouds and who supported the writing of this book every step of the way, thank you for letting me regularly sneak off to coffee shops to write when I would have otherwise been at my desk. And to Mom, who sparked me with all my creative impulses in the first place, thank you for always bringing me back to the arts.

To Rosemarie McKinnon of the Kinder Institute of Life Planning, your persistent and heart-forward encouragement helped me not only put pen to paper, but also pushed me to get this book across the finish line. Thank you for all your guidance and support in helping me develop my own "torch."

And finally, to my wife Naomi, I'm unsure if I even knew what purpose was before I saw you for the first time in a Montana airport. But from that moment, I knew that part of mine was to love you. Thanks for loving me back.

About the Author

Morgan is a singer-songwriter, an author, and the co-founder of Trailhead Planners, a financial planning and wealth management firm serving clients nationally. Morgan lives with his family in Minneapolis, MN.

You can find more information about Morgan and follow his blog at <u>morganranstrom.com</u>.

32838815R00095

Made in the USA
Lexington, KY
06 March 2019